SOUL
THERAPY

SOUL THERAPY

Joy Manné

North Atlantic Books
Berkeley, California

Published by
North Atlantic Books
P.O. Box 12327
Berkeley, California 94712

Cover art by Deborah Koff-Chapin
Cover and book design by Andrea DuFlon

Printed in the United States of America
Distributed to the book trade by Publishers Group West

Soul Therapy is sponsored by the Society for the Study of Native Arts and Sciences, a nonprofit educational corporation whose goals are to develop an educational and crosscultural perspective linking various scientific, social and artistic fields; to nurture a holistic view of arts, sciences, humanities, and healing; and to publish and distribute literature on the relationship of mind, body, and nature.

Library of Congress Cataloging-in-Publication Data

Manné, Joy.
    Soul therapy / Joy Manné.
        p.   cm.
    Includes bibliographical references.
    ISBN 1-55643-255-0
    1. Spiritual life. 2. Spiritual exercises. I. Title.
    BL624.M343 1997
    131—dc21   97-15002
                                                CIP

1   2   3   4   5   6   7   8   9   /   0 0   9 9   9 8   9 7

Soul does not need therapy.
We need Soul Therapy to learn
how to live on Soul-level.

I dedicate this book
to Sholem Manné, 1902–1952,
my almost unknown father,
and
to Vera Bergman Manné, 1921–1979,
my paradoxical mother

THE SOUL PATH OF THIS BOOK

Acknowledgments

A book about Soul Therapy has had Soul Therapy. Its spiritual parents are Dhiravamsa, who taught me meditation, and Hans Mensink and Tilke Platteel-Deur, who taught me Spiritual Therapy. During its many reincarnations, the manuscript had a sequence of sensitive midwives: Claudine Reymond, Gunnel Minett, Jane Ballantyne-Pearson, David Colbourne, Guus Oesterreicher, and Richard Grossinger. Gunnel Minett rebirthed it and is its godmother. David Colbourne is its godfather. Guus Oesterreicher and Alice Hulscher helped it to believe that this is a safe world to be born in. Hal and Sidra Stone gave encouragement.

During its various incarnations *Soul Therapy* has had several voices recognized—and some of the least user-friendly eliminated—in dialogues with Gunnel Minett, David Colbourne, and Richard Grossinger.

When the book was in its infancy, my daughter Janet gave some good guidance and my son Benjamin Lewis taught me that it was what I knew and not what I had read that people wanted to know. (I am a famous reading fanatic.) In its final incarnation, when I wondered if I would be writing this book forever, my spiritual daughter, Emma Webster, explained that "writing is rewriting." Somehow that made it easier. When it was almost grown up, my wise friend Gianna Grandi made just a few highly significant recommendations. When I could integrate all of these, the book was finished. Through its incarnations, as it tried each time to find its way into the world, Gunnel Minett, Gianna Grandi, Bo Wahlstrom, Wilfried Ehrmann, Guus Oesterreicher, David Colbourne, and Lynne Jenkins cheered it on and had faith in it. While I was in Berkeley, Professor Lewis Lancaster generously made available for me friendship, kindness, office space, and a computer so I could complete the project. Finally it was Roger Wicker who stood like Hermes at the crossroads and pointed the way.

We all need friends who believe in and encourage us. For many years Zamie Liknaitzky has told me—with wisdom, and with his unique brand of humor—that I could do it. I hope this book is part of what he meant that I could do!

I took a training in Spiritual Therapy with Hans Mensink and Tilke Platteel-Deur from 1985 to 1987. Those are the official dates. I continue to learn from their example every day and am eternally grateful to them for modeling a way of following the Soul Path that I hope I make my own. I do not know how to thank them enough. I am grateful too that it is possible for me to live a Soul Quest life with Johannes Bronkhorst, my husband. The name "Johannes" means "gift of God."

The case histories in this book are based on real case histories, with names, genders, and details disguised to protect the identity of the client, as ethics requires.

Everyone I have ever met, everyone who shared my Soul Path even for a moment, in whatever role—family member, friend or foe, supporter or competitor, teacher, therapist, student or client—has contributed to the experiences that eventually incarnated in this book. Thank you all.

CONTENTS

PART ONE

Ego Therapy and Soul Therapy

Ego and Soul

By *Ego*, I mean that part of the person that is conditioned and that is identified with being conditioned. Ego is a kaleidoscope of ever-changing energies: thought energies, emotional currents, instinctual forces, the energetic tensions in every personal history and in every nationality, the energy that sustains likes and dislikes, the energy of sub-personalities cooperating and conflicting. It is what we refer to when we say "I – me."

Ego seeks to find the meaning of its life: who it is, where it comes from, why it is the physical child of its physical parents, what lessons it is here to learn, what its life-task is. This is a Soul Quest.

Ego seeks its Soul Path because its task is a Soul Quest. It has to find its way to Soul, to communicate with Soul and to unite with it in order to know who it truly is. That way lies true happiness.

By *Soul*, I mean that part of the human being that cannot be described, but that can be sensed as perfect balance, absolute harmony, absence of all conflict and separation, full awareness, being centered, Unconditional Love, Peace, Truth. Sometimes it is called the Higher Self, sometimes Oneness. The Buddhists describe it as No-self, Unconditioned, Emptiness, Buddha

Nature, Already-Enlightened, or Perfect. When I look for a con-temporary expression, I call it the *inner shaman*.

Soul is energy too. When Ego is surrendered to Soul, Ego energies go quiet, and there is just flow: the flow of the right action at the right time doing the right thing. That is Soul Energy.

How do we recognize when Ego is surrendered to Soul? These are moments of intense harmony and peace. We watch a sunset: there is neither oneself nor the sunset; no separation, just oneness. We perform an action: there is no actor and no action; no separa-tion, just oneness. We make a decision: there is no opposition, there are no problems; it is as if the decision makes itself. We live our lives day by day, moment by moment: no separation, only oneness. Without conflict, and through this oneness, we "know." We know ourselves. We know others as they really are. We sense their energy-fields, know their thoughts, perceive their real inten-tions, recognize their Soul Quest. All the time we feel compas-sion. When the Ego is in communication with Soul, we honor the Earth and all beings.

Soul Therapy

Ego needs to understand. That is why Ego needs to describe Soul. When Ego believes it understands, it gets some sense of control and with that some sense of security. Soul just is. Soul already knows and understands Ego. Soul does not need to control Ego. Soul Therapy teaches Ego how to surrender to Soul. If Ego has nothing under its control, it will have nothing to surrender.

Ego-level and Soul-level are different energy states. Soul Therapy teaches us to distinguish between them so that we can increasingly live our lives on Soul-level.

Soul Therapy concerns all religions but is independent of any one of them. We use it to become truly religious.

Soul Therapy leads to effective communication between Ego and Soul so that we come to live in harmony and fulfill our life-tasks and our karma. This cannot happen unless Ego learns to function effectively, which means to know and sense Soul. Soul does not need therapy. We need Soul Therapy to learn how to live on Soul-level.

Protective and Creative Soul

Soul protects us from painful and traumatic experiences. It hides them from Ego until we are able to integrate them. What belongs to us but is hidden from us in our unconscious or withheld from us by Soul nevertheless has an influence on us. It pushes us to actions that go against our conscious wishes. It prevents us from choosing the direction of our lives. Like a car that drives its driver instead of the other way around, it is dangerous—dangerous for our work, dangerous for our relationships, dangerous for our success, dangerous for our creativity, dangerous for our happiness. The Soul Quest is dedicated to bringing to awareness and taking responsibility for these experiences because that way lie freedom and choice. As we develop autonomy, Soul has less protective work to do and its energy becomes free for other functions.

Soul not only hides our traumas: it is also our treasure trove. Soul has its own will. It directs our process of development. It has goals for us and lessons that it wants us to learn. It wants us to heal what needs to be healed in us. It wants us to recognize our destiny and to fulfill it. It pushes us to evolve. Soul connects us with other people, nature, and the whole universe. Soul is omniscient, divine, our Guide, our Wisdom, our Infinite Potential, our direct contact with God—in whichever way we understand that concept.

The Soul Quest

Throughout time, in all societies, Ego has always sought Soul and Soul has always made itself accessible to Ego. Regularly throughout time, different forms and methods of Soul-Questing, with differently described goals, have come about. Sometimes these have concretized into religions.

The way forms, methods, and goals of Soul-Questing are defined is always influenced by the cultures in which they arise.

This is important. Something that cannot really be described and that is not conditioned does not conform to any one description, or to any one method for finding or developing it. That is why Soul can be described in so many different ways and attained by so many different paths. These paths, however, have basic elements in common. The Soul Path is paved with Ethics. Sometimes these ethics are called commandments (Judaism and Christianity), sometimes The Noble Eightfold Path (Buddhism), sometimes rules for living well in a society (Confucianism). There are many different names. Every Soul Path method honors Ethics.

How can we talk about the Soul Quest if we all choose different words and cannot agree on a definition for Soul? It is so simple. I will use the words that have meaning for me; they are, after all, all that I have. Because Soul is transcendental, it will understand the words that come through me and will communicate their meaning in its own way to you. You would not have picked up this book if your contact with Soul had not guided you to it, and if Soul did not know there was at least something useful in it for you. There will be no problem in understanding because this book respects the uniqueness and the mystery of Soul. Ego seeks "rightness." It wants to control through knowing, but its idea of knowing is dualistic: it divides into right and wrong, mine and yours, this and not that. It wants to be on the one right way, and it wants other Egos to admit that *its* way is the one right way. That is why people who are lost in their Ego always think that their religion is right and all others are wrong, and that their way of living is right and all others are wrong, that their opinions are right and all others are wrong, etc. As there is no coercion to one point of view in this book, Soul will not need to protect Ego from it.

The words that I use to describe Soul may please or frustrate Ego, the "I – me" of the reader, and this may change in different parts of this book. *"I"* may like it. It may please *"me,"* or *"I"* may dislike it and it may displease *"me."* Both being pleased and frustrated are equally valuable. Ego is individual, and each Ego needs to get to know Soul in its own unique way. Soul does not mind. It is not attached to words or belief systems or religions; it is, however, religious in the best sense of that word, and profoundly and absolutely honest and ethical. If you are pleased reading this book, it is because through some wonderful chance, the words that I choose also speak to you. If you are frustrated, it can be because you would choose different words. In that case, this is an opportunity to find the words that best fit your way to sense Soul.

Soul-Questing

As long as there have been humans, Ego has sought Soul. The Soul Quest has had many different names. These days it may be called personal and spiritual development, personal growth, empowerment, humanistic or transpersonal psychology, humanology, or shamanism, among other expressions.

At all times for which historical records exist, in every civilization that has ever left traces of itself, the quest of Ego for Soul has been recognized. The positions of the figures in the art of cave people are templates through which particular altered states of consciousness can be attained.[1]

During some periods in recorded history, interest has been rather limited, while in others this quest has been widely respected and supported by society. It has been held to be the purpose of life. This is what happened in India between 600 and 400 B.C. when the great Indian religions came into being. The quest of Jainism was for liberation through non-action. The quest of Buddhism was for Nirvana, the unconditioned state. The quest of the secret teachings of the Upanishads was for knowledge of the true nature of the Self. Such questing on a large scale happened also around the time of the birth and life of Jesus Christ, and we are now in a similar current of energy. The Soul Quest interested only a very few exceptional people in the 1950s, became recognized by a limited public during the 1960s, was more generally accepted during the 1970s and widely recognized in the 1980s. Now, under a great variety of names, it is pursued by many people from all walks of life.

Carl Gustav Jung, who died in 1961, and who gave psychiatry the opportunity to (re-)become alchemy, was arguably the great predecessor of the contemporary interest in the Soul Quest. Besides Jung and his students, up to the 1950s, this search interested only a very few exceptional people like, for example, Aldous Huxley, Milton Erickson, Joseph Campbell, Alan Watts, Abraham H. Maslow, Fritz Perls, and Stanislav Grof. It began to be identified by ideas like "self-realization," "transpersonal," "transcendental," and with the desire to attain different altered states of consciousness and to live in a state of true consciousness. During the 1960s the Soul Quest became current among ever more diverse groups of people. Young idealists who followed pop stars like the Beatles took Love as their Path to development and a better world. They wanted only to love and to be loved and to be happy and they wanted everyone else also to love and to be happy, and they sang, "All You Need is Love." Also during this period, people started to rediscover ancient methods for achieving this goal. Increasing numbers of people on the Soul Quest started meditating. My own practice of Vipassana meditation began in 1965 with an inspired and forward-looking Thai monk. His title, as musical as a mantra, was then "Chao Khun Sobhana Dhammasuddhi," but since the 1970s he has called himself simply "Dhiravamsa." Dhiravamsa took Westerners, women as well as men, into his monastery and taught and inspired them.

Other ways to develop were explored. Some people experimented with powerful substances such as LSD, as well as those traditionally used in shamanic practice such as marijuana and mescaline, as part of their quest to extend their state of consciousness. For others the search for development and self-improvement was through the body, another traditional way. These questors experimented with vegetarian, macrobiotic, and other diets or began to learn yoga. Interest in altered states of consciousness, psychic abilities beyond those usually characterized as ordinary, and preventive medicine as opposed to the treatment of disease spread into the scientific and medical communities, which began to occupy themselves with the Soul Quest as a subject for research. The *Journal of Humanistic Psychology* was started in 1961. An Association for Humanistic Psychology was formed in 1964 in the U.S. and in Britain in 1969. The *Journal of Transpersonal Psychology* appeared in 1969 in the U.S.

During the 1970s, interest in the Soul Quest grew rapidly. Now also often called "self-realization" or consciousness, it was explored in new and different ways by Abraham Maslow, Robert E. Ornstein, and Ken Wilber, among others. New and powerful techniques came into being, including *Breathwork:* in many languages the word for breath and the word for soul are the same. The first book about Rebirthing by Leonard Orr and Sondra Ray, called *Rebirthing in the New Age*, appeared in 1977. Rebirthing is also called Conscious Connected Breathing or Conscious Breathing. Since then the use of conscious breathing techniques —including those related to the Japanese and Chinese martial arts and various forms of meditation and chanting—as a means for pursuing the Soul Quest has developed rapidly.

During this very productive period, Elizabeth Kübler-Ross studied problems related to the experience of dying. Ian Stevenson, Raymond A. Moody, and Morris Netherton studied the question of previous lives. O. Carl Simonton, Stephanie Matthews-Simonton, and James Creighton's seminal book, *Getting Well Again: A Step-By-Step, Self-Help Guide to Overcoming Cancer for Patients and Their Families,* was published in 1978. It became increasingly recognized that personality has an effect upon health and also upon the risk of developing particular diseases and of being cured or dying of these diseases. It became clear that we are not the *victims* of our character, but on the contrary, we are able to take it in charge and develop it in a positive direction. It became clear that we are able to—and indeed we must—use our character as a means for following our Soul Path, as a means for attaining physical and mental well-being. Personal and spiritual development continued to grow in recognition and respect. The Soul Quest also became an industry!

The 1980s saw further rapid growth of participation in personal and spiritual development and further research and inquiry in this field. At the beginning of this period, as if to herald it in, came Marilyn Ferguson's book, *The Aquarian Conspiracy: Personal and Social Transformation in the 1980s,* a detailed history of the contemporary evolution of interest in consciousness and its development. In a few countries, groups of people who had become so separated from the knowledge that the Soul Quest is a normal and eternal human activity took the idea of "conspiracy" literally, became suspicious, and tried to find the plot and plotters!

During this period, Bernie Siegel, a well-known oncologist, began to wonder why some people either recover completely from cancers that are supposed to be terminal, or die from them but die well. He wrote the Soul-nourishing book *Love, Medicine and Miracles* about this question. There was a proliferation of new methods and techniques of Soul-Questing and the "rediscovery" of what were claimed to be old ones. Awareness of the importance of myth in our lives became current wisdom. Michael Harner published *The Way of the Shaman.* People sought the ancient wisdom, interesting themselves in the sacred paths that were historically known to change consciousness positively, to facilitate personal and spiritual development, and to lead to transpersonal experiences.

If some of the new methods and techniques were genuinely effective, others were superficial, spurious in their origins, and more than doubtful in their purposes and results. The Soul Quest and the Ego Quest became confused. Many people threw themselves indiscriminately into whatever was labeled "personal growth" or "spiritual development." They followed all manner of gurus and pseudo-gurus. They became superstitious in their thinking, rejecting scientific thought and method in an extreme way. They went for expensive initiations or "attunements" of no proven authenticity, some of which promised to open capacities that either no one has or everyone has anyway, while others promised mastery of cosmic secrets *in only one week*—which turned out to be either meaningless and useless, or, in the better cases, to be only the basics of what is generally accepted in personal growth of the reliable kind. Other people fell for methods that made grandiose claims to turn them instantaneously into healers. There were workshops in which violence was justified! The names of the respectable sciences and disciplines of ancient civilizations were taken out of context and used to sell new inventions, with people of doubtful integrity inventing mythical origins in ancient India, China, Japan, or Tibet, or among American Indian tribes, to authenticate the most extravagant claims.

Good research, such as Jon Klimo's work on channeling, showed that everyone has the potential for abilities often called transpersonal: the mediumistic ability to hear "voices"; the ability to let healing energy flow through the hands; the ability to remember past lives; extrasensory perceptions and access to higher altered states of consciousness. Capacities formerly considered to belong only to certain peculiar people, and to be theirs only by chance, were shown to be inherent in everyone and available to be trained and developed, as with all talents such as playing a musical instrument or being able to paint, within the limits of individual differences and gifts.

Everything was new. Everything was inviting. Everything was exciting. How could one sort out what was available? How could one distinguish, before ever having tried, between what was of good quality and led to real and continuous development, and what was superficial and led nowhere? How could one learn to distinguish between what truly served the Soul Quest and what only served the Ego Quest? How could one be sure one was developing the *inner shaman* rather than the *inner charlatan?* There were no popular books, journals, or magazines that studied these new experiences seriously in a balanced and constructively critical way. In the excitement of freeing oneself from old constraints there was the idea that everything "worked," that every just-invented method led to genuine personal growth—in brief, that everything was for the best in the best of all possible worlds.

The result was that many people became disillusioned. They discovered that the experiences obtained here and there, in one workshop or another, the good feelings and powerful emotions that they felt for a while and that they enjoyed feeling, just do not last. They learned that although their experiences were strong and impressive at the time, nothing changed fundamentally in their lives: they did not become happier or wiser; their relationships did not improve in the long term; their sex lives did not become better; they did not find the job they longed to find; and they still could not express their creativity in the way they wanted to. They began to get a feeling for the difference between Ego Quest and Soul Quest. The 1980s saw the beginning of a constructively critical literature.

The creation of new techniques and the recovery of ancient ones, and the development of new knowledge and the recovery of ancient wisdom, continue. Interest in personal and spiritual development increases, and recognition of its value is ever wider. Its contribution to good mental and physical health is formally acknowledged, and new techniques are increasingly tested and integrated into health and medical services. The healthily critical spirit continues to grow. It is beginning to be recognized that the achievement and integration of transpersonal abilities and altered states of consciousness requires serious preparation. Historically, the groups of people who devoted themselves to Soul Quests of various kinds—the yogis, Buddhist meditators, Sufis, shamans from every tradition, and others—held the altered states of consciousness that are part of every Soul Quest in such high respect that they spent years in preparation to establish the solid foundation that these states require. We are now beginning to realize that if we really want to develop personally and spiritually there are no short-cuts, and that what is cheaply and superficially acquired at the beginning, in terms of time and commitment, and no matter what has been paid for it, will remain that always. The importance of a solid foundation is now recognized, as is the fact that when there is no foundation, the strong and sometimes disturbing experiences which characterize this work cannot be integrated and can be destabilizing.

We now have enough information and experience to consider the question, "How do we set about our Soul Quest in an effective way?" and to provide the contemporary answer—the answer of our own times. The Soul Quest is always contemporary. We cannot step in the same river twice. We cannot put new wine into old bottles. We cannot use old answers to *now* questions. It would be too easy and too dull: there would be no challenge and no quest if we could.

My Soul Path to Writing This Book

Some years ago, at the beginning of my practice as a therapist, a woman came to see me, accompanied by her husband. Let's call her Zoë. Zoë told me that she was depressed. She had consulted two psychiatrists who had pronounced that diagnosis and had prescribed drugs, which Zoë refused to take, with the result that the psychiatrists had refused to treat her any further. Most drugs given in psychiatry inhibit the Ego's quest for the Soul. Zoë was looking for a different way to come out of her depression, not an Ego-suppressing way, but a Soul Quest way.

Zoë was an attractive woman, curvaceous, always prettily dressed, responsible and independent. She had a very good relationship with her husband, a job, many hobbies, and a fine sense of humor. In fact, she had a rich and creative life. Her problem was that she was depressed and cried a lot, and did not know why. I agreed to work with her.

Then her husband asked me the question, "How do I know that you are not a charlatan?"

That is a good question. It is the right question to ask of all therapists no matter whether they come from the recognized and established trainings in psychiatry, psychotherapy, or counseling (because this gives no guarantee about their character, results, or level of personal and spiritual development) or whether they use the new methods and techniques.

I answered, "Give me three sessions with your wife and you will know." This was not casual arrogance on my part. I had met Zoë socially, had heard from her about her problem, and knew she had a strong enough character and a good enough life to be able to integrate the suffering that was overwhelming her at that moment.

His wife came out of her depression after the first session. No, I am not exaggerating. Zoë had suffered from a rare illness which necessitated many operations and which finally resulted in a hysterectomy, and she was not yet forty. She was sad, deeply and profoundly sad, and she was trying to repress this sadness. The result was that her sadness turned into depression. The painful memories of the many operations she had suffered were pushed away from consciousness, as were the memories of her childhood suffering. Respect and recognition are key aspects of all therapy: until we respect and recognize our suffering, we are controlled by the need to avoid it and so we cannot do the necessary grieving for our loss. Zoë needed to recognize and respect her sadness and to do her grieving in order to integrate these experiences. In this way she could come to accept them and to respect what they mean to her on every level of her life. Depression is a fixed, frozen, unchangeable, frightening state; sadness flows, and like everything that flows, it changes. The movement from depression to sadness is an important energy change: a change from Ego-energy to Soul-energy. Soul pain exists and it is holy.

Zoë and I did have more than three sessions together, and she developed very well. Her husband is convinced that I am not a charlatan.

I was impressed by the question, *"How can I know that you are not a charlatan?"* I thought about it a lot during the following year, because it was during that year that my Soul Path took me into the company of various people who offered new methods which purported to lead to personal and spiritual development, and who, I learned through painful experiences, really were charlatans! The question occupied my mind also because at that time my Soul Path brought me many clients who had suffered through being badly treated by therapists—practicing both recognized and new methods—who had not themselves achieved a sufficient level of personal and spiritual development and whose results were therefore both inefficient and destructive.

How do we get onto our Soul Path? How can we do our personal and spiritual development well? What, in fact, does it mean "to do it well"? How do we begin? How do we choose people to work with? How do we sort out the methods that lead to genuine and lasting development from those that belong to the charlatans: those that are fashionable for a moment, but that leave no lasting good results and may be dangerous and harm us? If we are doing it well, what should the results be?

My own Soul Quest had taken me into a training in *Spiritual Therapy* in Holland with Hans Mensink and Tilke Platteel-Deur. Hans and Tilke modeled the Soul Quest for their students. They led people through their fears and suffering onto and along their Soul Paths with gentleness, wisdom, and patience. I continue to be grateful every day that I took their training. The truly holy example that Hans and Tilke set continues to influence my work and my practice. I still call on my memories of their training for inspiration and guidance. Now they are my colleagues, but they will always be my Teachers. I honor them as my Teachers and as true Teachers of the Soul Path as well as therapists.

When I came to live in Switzerland, before I had even completed my training, people wanted to learn from me. In 1989 I opened a school, *École d'Évolution Personnelle et Spirituelle,* in which people could work on their own development and learn to accompany others doing the same. These questions acquired another focus as I became more experienced in teaching. In the beginning, when I asked myself why a certain student had not "got it" while others had, my attention was on how I could teach better. Gradually I noticed that some students came "with it," some "got it," some "had it" but would not commit themselves fully to practicing it, and others never "got it" at all. I remembered that it was no different in Hans and Tilke's training. What is more, I noticed that the students who "got it" were happier in every aspect of their lives. They were more ethical, more self-responsible, more joyful, more playful, and lots more fun—and so, quite obviously, had better relationships with themselves and others and more enjoyable jobs and lives.

When I eventually could name what the "it" was, I was able to write this book. I realized that the "it" that some people did not get was the step from Ego Therapy to Soul Therapy, from the Ego-path to the Soul Path, from the Ego Quest to the Soul Quest. Then I realized that what I needed to teach more explicitly was the difference between living on the Ego-level and consecrating one's life to Soul-level.

Not to Soul-Quest is Dangerous

Why does this have to be taught? Why should one "Soul-Quest"? Because anything less than that—anything less than consecrating one's life to Soul-level—is dangerous. *Not to Soul-Quest is dangerous:* dangerous to our health, dangerous to our well-being, dangerous to our happiness, dangerous to our relationships, dangerous to the achievement of our life task, and dangerous to our peaceful transition at death. Unless we are committed to our Soul Quest, we are dangerous to ourselves, dangerous to others, and dangerous to our planet.

Energy and the Soul Quest

For the perfectly healthy, idealized human, energy would flow unimpeded from cell to cell and radiate without interference in overlapping, and interrelated, fields. This perfect movement of energy would nourish the body and guide its many processes; would uplift, enlighten, and continuously inspire the mind; and would radiate outward, as love, into intimate connection with the surrounding world. Such a rare and fortunate person would feel good, *all of the time.*   —*Michael Sky,* Breathing *(p. 33)*

The Soul Quest is a quest to be part of freely flowing, pure clear energy. It is through energy awareness that Ego gets to know Soul. The subject of personal and spiritual development cannot be discussed separately from energy. When we do our personal and spiritual development well, our energy changes. We generate a different energy-field around us. Spiritual development is and has always been a question of becoming conscious of energy, disciplining it, training it, refining it, and purifying it. Ethics has always been basic to this process.

Developing means bringing the quality of our energy up to higher, finer, and more subtle levels. When we develop, our energy becomes more loving, generous, compassionate, and open. It becomes stronger, vaster, more extensive, more inclusive. It brings us beyond our preoccupations with our "little" self, our daily life, our personal survival, our individuality, and it joins us to the vaster energy and occupations of Soul, Self, Destiny, Transcendence, and the consciousness of Oneness with all existence. Hence comes our interest in and our sense of responsibility for the fate and well-being of our fellow inhabitants of this planet.

Energy is the theme of our times. Electronics, minute movements of energy, influence almost every aspect of our lives. The effectiveness of energy medicines like acupuncture, shiatsu, homeopathy, and osteopathy is becoming recognized even though these cannot yet be scientifically explained. New energy medicines such as electrocrystal therapy, vibrational medicine, and electrohealing are being explored. Energy Psychotherapy has not yet been written about formally under that title but it exists potentially already in several forms. The methods I write about—Breathwork, Voice Dialogue, and Past-life therapy—are Energy Psychotherapies. Rebirthing, or Conscious Breathing, is *par excellence* an Energy Psychotherapy, as is any method that uses the breath: breath being life and life being energy. Many methods now subsumed into the field of Somatics are Energy Psychotherapies. In the hands of a therapist who can help us get in touch with and recognize the energy of the complexes and the archetypes, Jungian analysis is also an Energy Psychotherapy. Bioenergetics, osteopathy, and the Chinese martial arts are Energy Psychotherapies, too. This is not an exhaustive list. Energy Psychotherapy, however, only becomes Soul Therapy when the therapist has access to Soul-level.

We are energy-beings. The human being is energy: the energy of the continually moving and changing atomic and sub-atomic particles that make up the body; the energy of the organs and of their functions; the energy of movements and activities; the energy of behavior, thoughts, attitudes, and intentions; the energy of every process. All of these elements contribute to creating a field of energy around each one of us. We transmit this energy and receive what others are transmitting to us. We are transmitters and receivers of energy.

Energy cannot lie or deceive. Our energy radiates from us and around us, informing others truly about what we feel and what we think. It tells others who we truly are. It transmits information about our quality as people: the quality of our mental and physical health, the quality of our functioning, how sexual we are, how intellectual we are, our level of personal and spiritual development—and everything else. Some people consciously and articulately read energy-fields. Others respond instinctively like animals. Whichever way other people react, with whatever degree of awareness, our energy-field has an effect upon our relationships with them and with the physical world.

The environment we live in is energy, too. Like us, everything on our planet and beyond it is energy: the energy of the continually moving and changing atomic and sub-atomic particles that make it up. We are energy-beings who are part of an energy-environment and who cannot be separated from it.

The Boomerang Law of Energy

The energy that we put into the world is a boomerang that we throw: it inevitably comes back to us. As we create and emit it, this energy creates the quality of our lives.

The people around us respond in accordance with the quality of our energy as we do in accordance with the quality of theirs. On days when we are "off" energetically—when our level of awareness is lower—we are out of control of our moods and our physical body. We are disagreeable to people and clumsy with the physical world. We disturb our family, friends, and colleagues; we stumble into things and break them; we injure our physical body. This does not happen on our good days. On our off days, our parents, children, boss, employees, colleagues, and everyone else we come into contact with responds by sending us the equivalent energy: by returning our awkward energy to us. They are impatient, insensitive, impolite, invasive, disrespectful, neglectful. On these days, we cannot achieve our goals. It is quite the opposite on a good day. Then we are at ease with the physical universe, and the people we come into contact with respond to us by supporting us in our needs and desires. They are sensitive, co-operative, appreciative.

The energy we put into our planet comes back to us, too. Abusing the environment is both self-abuse and abuse of all other beings. When the planet is abused through over-population, pollution, greed, callous exploitation, or the power-games of countries, individuals, or organized religions that have lost their original inspiration, we all suffer mentally and physically.

The Soul Path

There is a path that Ego follows in its quest to know Soul, the Soul Path. The Soul Path is a path of personal and spiritual development. There is no spiritual development without personal development. Ego achieves spiritual development through personal development.

Our Soul Path is a path that we have constructed for ourselves in our past from its eternal first moment through all of the choices that we made, and that we continue to construct in the present through each choice that we make, choices being a way of influencing and directing energy.

Spiritual development is traditionally called a path because development is like a journey. We each follow a path whose steps are unique, although paths have much in common. These steps are the tasks we have to perform and the lessons we have to learn on our Soul Path.

The Soul Path is a path of relationship: relationship with our selves and relationship with others. It is, after all, undertaken on this planet full of people. Usually we decide to encounter them. Sometimes we retreat from them for longer or shorter periods. The people we meet along our path accompany us for longer or shorter distances: some for a lifetime, some for the duration of a glance. All are potentially our teachers according to our ability to recognize this. The further we follow our path, the more we recognize and acknowledge the inner being and individual development of each other person and accept their role as our teacher, be it even for a moment.

We set forth upon the Soul Path by walking it. Personal and spiritual development do not just happen. It is work and we have to apply ourselves to it. Progress on the Soul Path is constructed step by step, like a building, and like a building, every aspect depends on the quality of its foundations. The quality and reliability of our progress on our Soul Quest and the firmness of our stance upon our Soul Path depend on our foundations: it is as genuine and trustworthy as they are durable. Constructing these foundations and following our Soul Path is work that is not taken up lightly. It is work that requires the greatest amount of sincerity and commitment.

Soul is not dualistic. It is harmonious and non-judgmental. On Soul-level, there is no right or wrong, only learning, only adjustment. On the Ego-level, right and wrong exist and we are more or less successful. We have more or less suffering, more or less happiness. Fortunately there are skills that Ego can learn in its Quest to contact Soul. These skills make following the Soul Path not only easier and less painful, but also *fun*.

There are more and less efficient ways for Ego to search for Soul. Basic on the Soul Quest are Ethics.

Ethics are not . . . a restriction, but a liberation. They are the way to realize our core nature and consequently are the path of truth and happiness. Moral codes are simply an approximate description of the life of a fully realized being. (p. 36)

[Ethics] are the voice of our buddha nature crying out from within. Our deepest nature wants us to live in harmony with the universe, because we are it and it is us. To act in an unethical way is to act against ourselves."   —*David Brazier,* Zen Therapy *(p. 39)*

Ethics will keep us on the path from Ego to Soul and prevent us from taking uncomfortable long-cuts.

Setting Forth

How do we set forth upon this path? Everyone who has ever asked themselves questions such as:

How can I develop?
How can I love myself knowing that my mother and/or father could not love me?
How can I express the love I have in me?
How can I become free from my feelings of being rejected and abandoned?
How can I rise above my fears and anxieties?
Why do I think and behave in ways that I know do me no good?
How can I develop self-esteem?

or questions about relationships, such as:

Why do my relationships always go wrong? How can I succeed in relationships?
Why do I repeat with my children what I blame my parents for doing with me?
How can I express my feelings?
How can I have a good sex life?
What work will enable me to express fully my gifts and my uniqueness?

or questions about personal abilities, such as:

> *How can I get in touch with my instincts?*
> *How do I become intuitive?*
> *How can I be spontaneous?*
> *How can I free my intelligence so that I can use it fully?*
> *How can I express my creativity?*

or questions regarding personal destiny, such as:

> *Who am I?*
> *What is the sense of my life?*
> *What is my real task in this world?*

or simply

> *How can I become empowered?*

or

> *Who or what is God / the Highest / Buddha Nature / the Soul?*
> *How can I manifest the inner shaman that I truly am in my life?*

. . . has already entered upon this Path—if he or she is really interested in discovering the answers.

Discernment

Someone asks us, "Do this, just for me." We do it, against our better judgment, and we live to regret it. We have let ourselves be manipulated. We did not have enough discernment.

We learn to be discerning. It comes with maturity and experience and with working on our process of development. Discernment enables us to distinguish between what is real and what is phony in every facet of our lives, and above all with regard to our Soul Quest. There is a lot on offer these days that purports to serve the Soul Quest. In the field of personal and spiritual development the abundance of methods, workshops, philosophies, and systems increases daily. To choose well we need to be discerning.

Discernment is acquired through life experience. It comes, too, through education. But above all, discernment comes through developing energy awareness. We have to learn to sense what is happening in our energy-field, what affects it, what influences it, what changes it: what makes it feel good and what makes it feel bad.

A book is by its own nature something of the mind: something that puts forward information, views, and theories. The role of information and education in the Soul Quest should not be underestimated: after all, knowledge is power. Knowledge has a very important role to play, but the Soul Quest does not take place on the intellectual level. The Soul Quest takes place on the energy level: it requires that we *sense* and that we *feel*. Sensations and feelings are responses to energy changes. Besides, the Soul Quest concerns eternal subjects like "Ethics" and "Love," about which nobody can say the ultimate word, and that learned and wise books have been written about from the time that writing was invented. As we advance on our Soul Path, our relationship with these eternal issues changes, and so it is an ongoing Soul Task to work out our relationship with them.

The Soul Quest is practical and experiential: if we don't *do* it, we just don't get it. There will be exercises in energy awareness throughout this book.

In this book you will discover aspects of my ability to discern: my values, the way I think, the teachers, methods, and books that have influenced me. I am writing *only* about how I, personally and individually, understand the Soul Quest. By reading this book, you are discovering my way—which is only one of many possible ways. Perhaps it appeals to you and convinces you completely, perhaps you find it only partially convincing, perhaps not at all. Each person has to find his or her own way. Each honest and ethical way is valid. *It's up to you to be discerning!*

However eternal the Soul Quest, the field of personal and spiritual development is relatively new in our recent history. There is not a great deal of objective information around. When we begin something, we have no experience: we are *at the beginning*. Yet unless we have had experience, how can we know how things should be or even know how things could be? On what basis do we discern? It is often difficult. Our lack of experience can lead to lack of confidence in our instincts, intuitions, and judgments. Where can confidence come from when we are inexperienced and at the beginning of our path of development? We seek and we are ignorant.

This is my proposal: take what I talk about in this book and use it as criteria. Develop the skills. Take the educational element as a basis and develop it too. Education is almost out of fashion these days, but there can be no doubt that the more informed we are, the better are our choices. Use your common sense and be practical. And take your mistakes positively: we all make mistakes and learn from them. Every path of development has sharp stones upon it, as well as soft grasses.

The Right Amount of Doubt

I recommend too the right amount of doubt. If we have too much doubt, we do nothing and do not progress. If we don't have enough doubt, we are credulous and superstitious and do not progress. Because we think in terms of "right" and "wrong," we tend to defend our decisions. Being "right" is so satisfying—but then we have nothing left to learn. Being "wrong" means losing self-esteem, and it can feel so bad. Both "right" and "wrong" are rigid positions. If we are limited to "right" or "wrong" we have no room to doubt. In between "right" and "wrong" is the vast area in which choice and alternatives exist, and it is there that we learn.

The Soul Quest is Fun

Life is a mystery and to Soul-Quest is to participate in this mystery. Sometimes this mystery is overwhelming in its wondrousness. Sometimes it is overwhelming in its fearfulness. Often we are not truly participating at all, just functioning, or—even worse—only surviving. Our schools give us little help. Our parents can teach us only to the extent they know. Our religions have forgotten. In any case, we do not want just to "function." We do not want merely to survive life, we want to *live* it. Deep down we know that there is magnificence, awe, wonder, glory, and that our rightful place is to be part of it. We know that life is a Holy Game and that learning its skills *is* our potential, if only we can find the right way. We *want* to be empowered to play this game to its limits and ours. Life-competence is within our potential and we want to attain it.

Learning skills is fun. Reaping the rewards of effort is fun. Moving from mere functioning to competence is fun. Somewhere deep inside we know that living this mystery fully is fun, wonderful fun.

Fun is serious, not trivial. Competence is fun; incompetence is no fun at all. Being empowered is so much more fun than blaming and victim-consciousness. Just watch the joyfulness of children as they learn their skills and become empowered. Fun is play, laughter, appreciation, enjoyment, spontaneity, generosity, joy, enthusiasm . . . all the wonderful things one can think of. Fun is *unobstructed energy*. Competence in life-skills is the best fun there is.

The word "therapy" does not conjure up images of fun. It is so earnest and so pain-related. Soul Therapy, like any other therapy, does bring up pain, and dealing with pain hurts. But that is not the center of Soul Therapy: its results are. Life becomes fun. Horizons open up. Energy becomes free. The result of Soul Therapy is the celebration of Life.

PART 2

Soul Quest Skills

The Soul Quest is an adventure, an opportunity to test our skills and to learn new ones. As good foundations hold a building steady, appropriate skills hold us steady through the hurricanes, volcanoes and earthquakes of our Soul Quest tests.

Tests can be scary. If the tests are worthwhile and if we are well prepared, they can also be fun. The Soul Path is ever more fun as we acquire the skills to tread it with confidence. Surprisingly, the skills are hardly difficult to acquire! Once we know what they are, and have the appropriate exercises, they are almost easy.

The Soul Path is paved with Ethics: the cement the paving stones are set into is Discipline. No skill is acquired without discipline.

None of the Soul Quest skills are definitively acquired, and none of the tests on the Soul Path are definitively passed. It is always possible to go further.

ONE
Skillful Ethics

The Soul Path is paved with Ethics. If we are not living an ethical life, we are not following a Soul Path.

In Ethics, the Boomerang Law of Energy is sometimes called karma, the process of reaping the consequences of our actions. Sometimes it is expressed "an eye for an eye, a tooth for a tooth." There are people who make the terrible mistake of taking this as permission to take revenge and do harm. What this expression describes is what happens *to us* when we perform good or harmful actions. Ethics can be summed up in the idea of *not harming*: not harming ourselves, not harming others, not harming the planet we live on, and not harming the universe we live in. Harming can never be justified and inevitably brings harm back. The boomerang that we throw always comes back. Skillful ethics means consciously creating good energy all of the time.

Here is an ethics exercise to help you experience the relationship between your practice of ethics and your energy-field.

Ethics Energy

- *Take up your usual position for inner work: any position that is comfortable for you: sitting, standing, or lying down. Close your eyes.*

Part 1

- *Imagine that you have nothing at all to reproach yourself with, nothing at all to feel guilty about, no regrets at all. No matter how far back you look through your life history: today, yesterday, last year, your childhood, your gestation, your conception and even before that, imagine that there is nothing whatever that you wish you had not done.*
- *How do you feel? Can you sense lightness, clarity, an unobstructed energy-field? Are you in touch with your body? How does your skin feel? Your head? Your back? Your belly? Are you physically comfortable?*

Part 2

- *Now go back to this morning and take stock of your day. Is there anything that you do have to reproach yourself for? Is there anything that you feel guilty about, or that you wish you had not done?*
- *Now how do you feel? Has anything changed in your energy-field? How does your body feel? Your skin? Your head? Your back? Your belly? What about your feeling of physical comfort now?*

Part 3

- *Repeat Part 1. End on a high note. Always finish in good energy. That is a basic energy maintenance skill.*

Someone who cannot feel the difference between Parts 1 and 2, is either a completely enlightened being, or completely possessed on the Ego-level, a danger to themselves and to everyone and everything on the planet.

Religions give us guidance in ethics. Because the original purpose of each religion, which is guidance for following the Soul Quest, has so often been forgotten, their advice has been seen as limiting rather than liberating. Religions are means of Soul-Questing that we use according to our character and wisdom.

Judaism offers us the Ten Commandments:

*1. I am the Lord your God, . . . you shall have no other gods before
me.*
*2. You shall not make for yourself an idol in the form of anything in
heaven or on earth.*
3. You shall not misuse the name of the Lord your God.
4. Remember the Sabbath day by keeping it holy.
5. Honor your father and your mother.
6. You shall not murder.
7. You shall not commit adultery.
8. You shall not steal.
9. You shall not give false testimony against your neighbor.
10. You shall not covet what belongs to other people.
—Exodus 20:2–17.

We understand the concept "God" according to our religious
inheritance and preference, and the times we live in. Once the idea
of a masculine god was prevalent. Now we have a wider view. We
personalize God as both masculine and feminine. The idea of
"God" also means the Soul Quest. An authentic belief in God
cannot be taught. It can only be achieved through Soul-Questing.

The danger of creating destructive energy is described in these
commandments too:

*I, the Lord your God, am a jealous God, punishing the children for
the sin of the fathers to the third and fourth generation of those that
hate me, but showing love to a thousand generations of those who
love me and keep my commandments.*   —Exodus 20:5.

When we create destructive energy we bring suffering to all of
those near to us; when we create good energy we do this for the
benefit of the whole planet. If enough good energy is created we
will eventually have a happy and healthy planet.

Jesus and other Jews of his time simplified the ten into just two
commandments:

*1. Love the Lord your God with all your heart and with all your soul
and with all your mind.*
2. Love your neighbor as yourself.   —Matthew 22:37–39.

Again, it is up to each of us to understand the concept of "God" according to our means.

Jesus also said,

> *Anyone who breaks one of the least of these commandments and teaches others to do the same will be called least in the kingdom of heaven, but whoever practices and teaches these commands will be called great in the kingdom of heaven.*   —Matthew 5:19.[2]

Some people understand "the kingdom of heaven" literally. It can also mean the quality of life that we create for ourselves moment by moment here on Earth through following a moral and ethical path, a Soul Path.

Buddhism offers us a code of conduct called the Noble Eightfold Path to the Cessation of Suffering. This comprises:

> *Right View,*
> *Right Thought,*
> *Right Speech,*
> *Right Bodily Action,*
> *Right Livelihood,*
> *Right Effort,*
> *Right Mindfulness,*
> *Right Concentration.*

The paths above are paths of ethics and discipline. In Soul Therapy, being ethical is being psychologically healthy.

> *In Zen, ethics are not simply a matter of setting boundaries to life, or to the therapy process. They are, rather, the central nub of the therapeutic problem. To be psychologically healthy is to return to and live from our core ethics.*
> —*David Brazier,* Zen Therapy. *(p. 44)*

It is not only religions that offer us guidance for following the Soul Path, but political movements like the Greens, idealistic philosophical movements like the one now called the "New Age" (in its best sense), psychological or growth movements like the Human Potential Movement, and also therapies that place an emphasis upon discipline and ethics: Rebirthing or Conscious Connected Breathing and Voice Dialogue, among others. Some people are born with the qualities necessary for following the Soul Quest. Most of us need therapy and spiritual disciplines to help us develop and practice these qualities.

Skillful Integrity

The Soul Quest is either wholly followed or not followed. Every compromise in morality or ethics takes us away from our Soul Quest. Integrity means walking our talk.

Ethics Test: Do you walk your talk?

Part 1

• *Go back to the beginning of today and review your day. How many things did you do that you wish you had not done? Can you feel as you think of them how these actions that betrayed your integrity break up and disperse your energy-field?*

Part 2

• *Now go back again to the beginning of today, and for each time you went against your better judgment, imagine a better, more authentic way for you to complete the event. Clear up your day and your energy-field in this way. How does your energy-field feel now? How do you feel now?*

TWO
Skillful Self-Responsibility

The entrance to the Soul Path is Self-responsibility, and we are only on this path as long as we are self-responsible. The Soul Quest is beyond the capacities of people who are unwilling or unable to be self-responsible. It is always our own responsibility to decide to follow the Soul Quest and to choose how we follow it. No one can do that for us. No one can shove or push or persuade us into Soul-Questing.

Skillful self-responsibility means that we treat every event in our lives as an opportunity for Soul-Questing. Usually we give more attention to unpleasant than to pleasant experiences, but we can equally learn from pleasant experiences. When we learn from pleasant experiences we increase our ability to have fun in life. When we are Soul-Questing we ask ourselves questions like:

- *"How did I create this experience?"*
- *"What do I have to learn from it?"*
- *"How does this experience serve my development?"*
- *"What could I do differently to be sure to repeat / to avoid such an experience in the future?"*

These questions put us into the driver's seat of the car that is our life and advance it on its route. There are no dead ends on the Soul Path. It only feels like that when we do not ask ourselves the right questions.

Mental Archaeology

Asking ourselves the right questions is Mental Archaeology. Once we have discovered a useful question we use it to uncover the thought and behavior patterns that we are not conscious of, just as brushes, spades, and shovels are used in archaeology. It is an Energy Law that when we are aware of a behavior pattern it changes of itself: positive patterns become even more positive; negative patterns stop controlling us.

In Mental Archaeology the basic techniques are the Listing Technique, the use of Affirmations, and Creative Visualization. These techniques can be used together. They are mutually supportive.

The Listing Technique

First decide on the question you are going to use. Then write it at the top of a page, or speak it into a tape recorder if you prefer. It is important that you record your question and your answers. Write down your responses as soon as you think them, and as fast as you can, without censorship and without judgment. Just let them flow and record them. If no response comes, or if only a few come, it is a good idea to repeat the phrase aloud a few times. That can open the flood gates.

Eventually you come to an answer that is the "big one." You know which one it is because your energy changes. You sigh, laugh, cry, get angry, see the light, feel relieved. The time to stop the process is when there has been an insight or a release of energy. There is no point in overdoing it. Some questions carry so much information for us that we come back to them again and again. We cannot usually reveal the whole of a physical archaeological site in one session, and mental archaeological sites too take time to excavate.

Sometimes answers do not come. This may be because the responses to the question you are using are not available to you where you stand on your Soul Path at that moment. It may also be that the question is wrongly worded. If you repeat a question about four or five times and no response, or no further responses come, all you can do is accept it. That is how your path is at the moment. Surrender and move on.

This technique can be applied to phrases as well as to questions.

These phrases can be related to our pleasant or unpleasant experiences. I suggest you use as many pleasant ones as unpleasant ones. So often therapy is focused on our suffering because we want it to stop, and that is sensible, after all. It is also useful to do mental archaeology on our successes. That way we become conscious of how we created them, and then we are empowered to create more of them. If we give our energy to creating successes, there will be much less of it available to go into suffering.

Here is an exercise to practice the Listing Technique. It uses a repeated phrase.

Listing Exercise

- *Think of a recent experience. It can be a good one or a bad one.*
- *List whatever comes into your head in response to the phrase:*
    —One way that I created this experience is . . .
    —And another way that I created this experience is . . .
    —And another way . . .

Example

- *I go to my mother for tea. She makes me the chocolate cake she used to make on birthdays when I was a child. It is years since she has done that. We have a wonderful afternoon together. I come home and wonder why this cannot happen every time I am with my mother. I decide to explore this. I use the phrase above and I list my answers.*

    Some answers that come up are:
    —by phoning my mother at a time she finds appropriate.
    —by telling her good news.
    —by not getting into our usual controversies.

There are many further opportunities to practice listing with questions and phrases in this book.

The Use of Affirmations

The use of affirmations is based on the idea that our thoughts are creative. An affirmation is a statement in which we affirm something is true that we would like to be true about ourselves or in our lives but which is not yet true. It is a way of substituting a positive thought for a negative one. Affirmations always open the door to more pleasant experiences. The use of affirmations can be supported by visual techniques like creative visualization: we support our affirmations by visualizing our pleasant, ideal outcomes.

Here is a simple example. It seems to many people that the essential missing ingredient in their life's happiness is a partner to share their life with. Caroline was lonely and in despair about finding a partner. Her negative thought pattern was, "I'll never find a partner who can offer me a good relationship." And truly she did not. She found any number of partners who could offer her a not-good relationship. Caroline then worked on the affirmation, "The partner who can offer me a good relationship is now coming into my life." This thought changed her attitude towards the people she met. Instead of being pessimistic and negative about all the people she met, she began to have positive expectations. Everyone she met was a potential ideal partner. Affirmations can be used on Ego- or Soul-level. Caroline started with an Ego-level wish to be happy. Her affirmation opened her up to the Soul-level thought that everyone we meet is potentially our partner in a good relationship. She began to see the value of each of her encounters with other people.

The idea that thoughts are creative can lead to foolish and superstitious thinking. When this idea is misunderstood, people believe that if only they make an affirmation frequently enough, what they affirm will inevitably come to pass. A client called Edgar, who had high educational attainments and held a responsible job in a bank, wanted to change his job. Edgar had taken many courses in positive thinking. As part of his effort, he told me, he was working with an affirmation, which he was writing hundreds of times a day. "But what do you *do?*" I asked him. "Do you look in the newspapers? Have you been to a job agency?" Edgar looked at me with eyes like saucers. "You mean I have to *do* something?" he asked. Of course we need to cultivate a positive frame of mind or we get nowhere, but let's avoid being silly.

An affirmation is a tool for self-analysis. We repeat the phrase, often by writing it, and we observe the negative thoughts and the painful memories it brings up. We feel the emotional distress. Gradually the repetitions reveal what is underneath, sometimes like the use of a heavy spade in archaeology, sometimes like the use of a gentle brush.

A favorite example in many facile self-help books is the banal affirmation, "I am now becoming a millionaire." How could using this affirmation be helpful? Money problems are connected to self-esteem and empowerment problems. If we use this affirmation, we may discover this sort of sequence of answers:

- *But my father told me I would never be any good at making money.*
- *But if I become a millionaire my whole family will be after me to support them, and I give them enough as it is*
- *But no one in our family has ever become rich or even comfortable.*
- *But my religion tells me that money is dirty and sinful.*
- *But what I really want to do is give all my property away and become a Buddhist nun.*

Eventually there is an energy change and we discover the thought that is controlling us. With regard to money, there are usually many of them. Even if we discover all of our negative thoughts on this subject, it does not mean that we will instantly become millionaires. It just means that our negative thoughts about money will no longer get in the way of our business ventures. We still have to invent the way or learn the skills that enable us to become the millionaire that we wish to become . . . and then to use our riches on Soul-level!

Creative Visualization

Creative Visualization means putting images to our affirmations. We create in detail in our minds the outcomes of our affirmations, as if we were projecting images onto a television screen.

Georgina wanted desperately to form a long-lasting partner-
ship, resulting in marriage and children. During a Breathwork
session I asked her to imagine that the man of her ideals was
standing outside the door, and to ask him to come in. Her
response was simple and instant. "No!" she said spontaneously,
and realized that she was not yet ready to let the man of her ideals
into her life. A year later she was living with her ideal man and
now they are married. Awareness is so empowering!

Creative visualizations test our negative thoughts visually, just
as affirmations test them verbally. They show us where we are
using our energy to block what we think we want, rather than letting it come to us. Once we are aware of our conditioning, it no
longer controls us.

How Self-Responsible Are We?

That our thoughts are creative is basic to the idea of Self-responsibility. Self-responsibility, however, should not become an
extreme or a fanaticism. It certainly does not mean denying the
role that other people play in our lives. In the drama of our life,
there are other characters on stage, not just ourselves.

Self-Responsibility Test 1: How self-responsible are you?

- *Think of a difficult and painful experience that happened to you
  recently and which made you suffer. Can you see your part of the
  responsibility for what happened, however painful it is for you to
  admit it?*
- *Are you responsible for what happened to you or not?*

If your answer to my question is "No, not at all," *this is your way
of choosing not to be self-responsible.* Someone or something
"other" than yourself or "outside" your control was responsible
and you had therefore no possibility, no means, no power to control or to choose anything whatever in the situation. You are
choosing a belief that places you firmly into the role of the victim.
Victims may have more or less power to manipulate people, but

they have no honest power and are thus incapable either of learning or of changing. If you are choosing the role of victim, you are choosing a state of spiritual powerlessness—even if your manipulations work!

If your answer to my question is "Yes, absolutely!" either you have a very clear example, or you are inflated and unrealistic. Most of our interactions involve other people and things, and it is most unlikely that we can control everything.

If your answer is "Yes, for my part of it," *you are choosing to be self-responsible in a realistic way.* Your part is the only part you can be responsible for.

I very carefully said in the test, "Can you see *your part* of the responsibility for what happened?" I limited your responsibility to *your part* because I want to avoid extremes. I especially avoided asking, *"Are you responsible for everything that happens to you in your life or not?"* Like so many good ideas, the popular idea that "thoughts are creative" and that we are responsible for what happens to us in our life can be taken to extremes. Other people exist and they too have responsibility. In the dance of relationships there is a "to and fro" between ourselves and others. Ego thinks that we can control every event in our lives through our thoughts. That way Ego deludes itself that it is divine! Soul already is divine. It has no need for this delusion.

How Thoughts Create Situations

How are thoughts creative? Here are some examples:

- *Frank always talks in a voice too low to be easily heard. In this way he succeeds in irritating his parents, his wife, his children, his employer, you, and me. Frank has the thought, "I irritate people," and he is successful at proving to himself that this thought is right.*
- *Gerald always arrives an hour late when he is invited to eat with his mother, and each time she complains. In this way he succeeds in spoiling their evenings together and in ensuring that the relationship between them remains tense. Gerald has the thought, "My mother never wanted me." Unconsciously he works to make this thought true.*

- *Henry has always asked his father to lend him money, from his childhood, through his adolescence, and right up to the present. And Henry is forty now. In this way he regularly gives his father the chance to interfere in his business and his way of life, and he creates opportunities for himself to exasperate his father. His negative thought is, "My father thinks I am no good," and he works hard to prove that this thought is true.*

We can also set ourselves up for pleasant experiences:

- *Caroline was deeply and respectfully loved by her father. Her conviction is, "All men love and respect me." She is surrounded by good and loyal men friends and colleagues, lives in a happily monogamous relationship with her devoted husband, and her sons adore her.*

These examples of familiar situations show how we create painful and pleasant experiences through our expectations. These are our hidden agendas. We are not conscious of what we are doing, otherwise—with regard to the painful experiences, at least—we would not do it.

Self-Responsibility Test 2: Do you have a hidden agenda?

- *Think again of the difficult and painful experience that happened to you recently and that made you suffer.*
- *Now write on the top of a sheet of paper,*
    "A reason that I (do a type of behavior) is . . . "
  and, using the Listing Technique, write the first thing that comes into your head.
- *Then think or say aloud,*
    "Another reason that I — is . . . "
  and again write the first thing that comes into your head.
- *Keep going for about ten minutes and you will surprise yourself.*
- *Do you have a hidden agenda?*

Example

Frank might write on the top of his page,
  "The reason that I talk so quietly that no one can hear me is . . ."
and some of the answers he may discover are:
  —because I am shy.
  —because I feel worthless.
  —because that way I get more attention.
Gerald may discover that he is punishing his mother.

Through this exercise we can test the extent of our role in each situation. Hidden agendas are Ego-level. Even when we are not conscious of them, they are ways we have of manipulating others.

The Dance of Relationships

Relationship is a dance. Whatever the relationship, the steps that we dance influence the steps that others are able to dance with us, and their steps in turn influence our dance with them.[3] If we believe that we are not loved, we will provoke in others a response that confirms our belief: we will do things in order to lose their love.

This is how Helen dances. Helen works in an office as a secretary. There she regularly makes mistakes and shows herself to be clumsy and incompetent, while the truth is that she is intelligent and well-trained. It is as if the faults and errors happen through her and in spite of her. Most of the time her work is rather good, and then suddenly, and usually at the most inconvenient moment, she makes mistakes. Helen is conscious that this happens. She is also unhappy because she recognizes her responsibility in the situation. Nevertheless, she is incapable of preventing herself from doing it—like a person who drinks too much and knows that she drinks too much, and yet continues to drink. Helen has been convinced since her earliest childhood that she is clumsy and incompetent. She continues today to create situations to prove to herself that she is right: that she is *in fact* clumsy and incompetent. Helen will continue to set herself up in this way until she becomes conscious of the thoughts that are responsible for her actions. Until then, her steps in the dance of relationships will force people to see her as clumsy and incompetent.

To take skillful self-responsibility for a behavior pattern, we have to become conscious of it. This is the necessary step that takes us beyond its control.

THREE
Skillful Character Management

Self-responsibility has sub-tests. One of these is our Character. We are surely tested by our character.

We are born with a program which we call our character, in a setting—our family, society, and country—that influences our development. We have personality from at least the moment of conception. Mothers observe differences in the behavior of their babies in the womb. Astrologers read our character in our birth charts and discover the origin of many of our tendencies through studying the charts of our families. Some people claim that we are influenced by our past lives or by our birth trauma. If we are on an Ego-path, we accept this passively and believe we have to live with it and that others have to make do with it too and to live with us as we are. If we are on a Soul Path, we take it as a challenge.

Our character is the way we think and act. It is also our body, through which we manifest who we are and what we are like physically. Through any number of possible circumstances—birth trauma, past lives, destiny, karma—each of us has one or several basic existential negative thoughts or beliefs. These might be beliefs about the nature of life, such as, "Life is dangerous," or "I must fight to survive," or "I have no right to exist." They might be beliefs about other people, such as, "I can't trust anyone," or "Nobody loves me." They might be beliefs about ourselves, such as

"I will never succeed," or "I am not good enough." Unfortunately, many people have the thought, "I don't want to be here on Earth."

These negative thoughts seem so obvious and self-evident to us that we never question them. Like post-hypnotic suggestions, they live in our unconscious and we spend our time acting them out. We create a reality that corresponds to them. Psychoanalysis calls this the "repetition compulsion."

Yvonne is born into a very poor family in which there is never enough money for food and where the children cannot be given a good education. Yvonne's parents do not have time for her because they work day and night, and besides, they have several other children. This type of situation is difficult to bear for any child. In her unhappiness, Yvonne thinks: "There is never enough for me." In time, through her strength and will, Yvonne succeeds in creating a good life for herself. She gets an education at evening classes; she creates her own business; she becomes very successful; she becomes very rich; she marries happily; she has everything she ever wanted and more. Nevertheless, all the while she continues to be afraid of not having enough, and this fear causes her great suffering. Yvonne does not question the truth of her thought, "There is never enough for me," because she is not conscious of it. She cannot relax and enjoy her financial success and her relationship. She is unable to notice that there is money enough and to spare, and that her husband spends lots of time with her. The old thought that rules her way of looking at life makes her blind to reality. Yvonne is living in the past and not in the present. We all know people like Yvonne, people who have a lot but don't seem to know it, so that they live in fear and poverty and dissatisfaction in the middle of their plenty. The "poorest" person I ever knew drove a Rolls Royce!

Our personal negative thought is a key to the lessons we have to learn on our Soul Path. It is a meditation subject, a form of *koan*.

Koan is a Japanese word for the tests life presents us with: problems not amenable to simple logical solution. Koan practice is meditation in which one holds such a dilemma in mind with great intensity, trying

to break through to new clarity. "New clarity" does not necessarily
mean a solution. It means a new view of life which arises when the
blocked energies within us find a way of release.
                    —*David Brazier,* Zen Therapy *(p. 46)*

The use of a koan is a way of breaking free from habitual patterns
of thinking and limiting belief systems. This personal negative
thought is a Soul Quest test. Our task is to learn that it is not true.
A person who thinks, "I must fight to survive," has to learn that
there are ways of responding to situations other than fighting. A
person who thinks, "I am not good enough," has to learn that
they really are good enough. We also have to learn how this negative thought serves our Soul Path. Joanna's koan is "I am not
good enough," and she used to believe it literally with absolute
conviction. If she were good enough, her father would not have
left her mother and her mother would not have loved her other
siblings more than she loved her. Therefore she was not good
enough. Joanna is a warrior: her inner shaman was born strong.
Quite instinctively, because of her nature, she took this idea as a
challenge. She determined to become good enough. When she
came for therapy she already had many qualifications and a satisfying job. Now she was going to learn how to make a good intimate relationship: she was going to become "good enough" to be
somebody's favorite person. It was great fun when Joanna discovered how her personal negative law had worked in her favor. It is
still her koan. Whenever this belief comes up now, she takes it
positively. "Oh ho," she says to herself, "I have more to do." And
she gets on and does it. Joanna has transformed her erstwhile negative thought into a useful guide for her Soul Path. It reminds her
that she *is* good enough.

We are free to change our thoughts and we regularly have to.
Change is the essence of Soul-Questing.

To change can be a frightening idea. It so often connected with
disapproval, our own and that of others. We *have* to change
because something about us—grades, hairstyle, efficiency at

work, weight, skill at relationships or communication—is not good enough. We are not loved as we are. To change can feel like submitting to other people's values and our own sense of inadequacy. If our motive for change is others' requirements of us, change is self-betrayal.

Change is also frightening because it carries no guarantees. The people who want us to change have not promised to love us if we change according to their requirements, and indeed they cannot make this promise. Even if we seek to change for our own happiness, we may fear the outcome once we are different. We will have to learn to live with ourself in its new form. Change is a risk.

Change requires self-confidence. We have to trust that if we take the risk we will not diminish our resources, but will indeed find more and better ways to become happy.

Self-Responsibility Test 3: How willing are you to change?

Part 1

- *Write down as fast as you can all your negative thoughts about yourself. Write for a maximum of three minutes, or fill not more than half a page.*
- *Now, sort these thoughts into categories.*
- *Take the strongest expression in the largest category and turn it into its opposite.*

Example

- *Suppose you come to the thought "Nobody loves me." Use the thought, "The world is filled with people who love me."*
- *How willing are you to let the new thought become your way of looking at the world?*
- *What might you lose if you do?*

Part 2

- *Write down as fast as you can all your positive thoughts about yourself. Write for a minimum of six minutes, or fill not less than two pages. It's always good to end on a high note, and it is skillful energy maintenance, too.*

A word that I prefer to "change" is *"exploration."* Soul-Questing is exploring, and to change is an adventure in new possibilities. The essence of any adventure is that we do not know its outcome in advance. Sometimes in therapy we feel guilty as we discover our share of the responsibility for our suffering and that of others. The ideas of *exploration* and *adventure* can save us from this. When we undertake an adventure—and life is the greatest adventure—we know in advance that it is not possible to "get it right" all of the time. By the rules of adventures, we are free to make mistakes, to learn and to change. We just hope we will get it right enough times to succeed! The outcome of our Soul Quest is not known in advance. We learn what it is as we reap its rewards.

The Temptation to Blame

What is our responsibility when people are unkind to us? What about cases of abuse and mistreatment? Surely people who have hurt us are responsible and *should* be blamed and punished? It is a hard lesson to learn—and sometimes it feels unjust—but such thoughts have no part in a Soul Quest. Blaming ourselves or others takes us off our Soul Path and into the role of victim—a role that can feel so comfortable and self-righteous.

Sometimes we blame ourselves for our suffering and beat ourselves up. Usually we blame our parents, those modern-day scapegoats. We say, "It is because my father was always absent that my relationships with men never succeed," or we complain about our father's weakness, his anger, or his other faults, and we blame him for our problems. We say, "It is because my mother preferred my brother/my sister/my father/her work that I always feel abandoned and rejected," and we blame her for our problems. Sometimes we blame our education and our society. We say, "It is because the education in my country is rigid and without imagination that I cannot express my creativity and be successful," and we blame it for our problems. Blaming is boring and repetitive.

Frederick, when he was over fifty, screamed at his aged mother that she was the source of all of the problems in his life. His parents had been paying for therapy for him since he was nineteen. No matter what his parents had done wrong in his youth, Frederick at over fifty is a "big boy" now. If all the therapy that he has had over the years is not working, he is old enough to realize that the problem lies with him.

Most parents have done their best. There are really very few who set out consciously to wound their children. Many adults complain that they did not get unconditional love from their parents. I say, let us stop blaming. If we know that unconditional love is important, let us start by giving it to our parents. Let us discover whether we ourselves are capable of giving it, before we demand that someone else should give it to us.

The "blaming" way of justifying our problems is not convincing. In our own family we observe that our brothers and sisters have different reactions to shared experiences. They do not view our parents, school, society, or each other in the same way that we do. They do not have the same problems. With courage we can accept that these reactions come from our individual character, with its peculiarities and uniqueness. Then we can work to change our unsuccessful thoughts and behavior. In this way we become free.

When we blame we disempower ourselves. Even in the most shocking cases of abuse, no matter how awful our parents were, by the time we are adults and they are wiser, they cannot change much for us. They cannot put the clock back, however much they may wish to. If we are lucky and our parents are strong enough to talk about our experience of childhood and to listen to our side of the story, they can help us through their love and support. If we are generous enough to do the same for them, then parents and children can proceed together on the Soul Path.

Some years ago I worked with two women, both of them in their early fifties. Each one had been severely abused by her parents. One refused outright to take responsibility for herself; the other took it completely. Each of them had had years of therapy before coming to see me. Let's call them Anne and Brenda.

Anne started by telling me that her goal in coming to me was to become happy. She had a very encouraging first Conscious

Breathing session. No sooner had the session begun than she experienced herself surrounded by and bathed in strong white light. Anne was astonished and moved. She told me that although she had been practicing her religion all her life, this was the first time that she had ever felt close to God. After a while her experience changed and became a gentle encounter with the shadow. She had a vision of small devils. Although her religion might lead her to fear devils, she did not fear these. They were happy and playful and she did not feel at all endangered. These healing visions and images showed Anne the path that her development would follow: a path on which she would be in strong white light and on which she would also safely meet her shadow, which was not dangerous.

In her next session Anne refused to work with her breath. Instead, she began to complain about her mother, whom she blamed for all of her problems. Her monologue went on for a long time, uttered like a quotation of several pages learned by heart, and I wondered how many times she had spoken it before in exactly the same way. Finally it came to an end and she announced in conclusion, "I am not ready to cut my umbilical cord; I am not ready to separate from my mother," pronouncing these phrases with great satisfaction. It was evidently an irrevocable decision. I asked Anne, "What will happen to your mother if you become happy?" "My mother will be really happy," was her instant reply. "Anne, you are fifty," I said, "stop taking revenge on your mother. Stop punishing her and start to take responsibility for yourself. Build your own life. It is the only way that our work together will succeed. Working with your breath is easy and fruitful for you. You have already had a good experience. That is the direction of your development. Let's go on with it and see where it will lead you next."

Anne never came back. Sadly, it was important for her to go on blaming her mother.

Brenda, the second woman, had no interest in blaming her parents. She wanted to heal her suffering and to become free. Her goal was to make up for her lack of education so that she could find work where she could be of use to others. Brenda wanted to take responsibility for herself as completely as possible. With such an attitude she could only succeed.

Blaming is a circular process, a vicious circle: We feel injured. We blame. We are self-righteous. We want to punish the people who have hurt us. We are so much holier than they are! We are possessed by the illusion that we are entitled to revenge. Now we are captives. We are the prisoners of our problems in this vicious circle: we have to maintain them because they justify our wish for revenge. But to advance on our Soul Path we have to let go. There is no place for vengeance on a Soul Quest. If people hurt us, it may be because we have at some time created the energy space for them to do so through our actions in this or in a past life. It may also be because our energy space is not clear enough. We need to develop sufficient understanding to perceive that all hurtful actions come from pain. Then we will be able to observe them with gentle compassion, rather than to suffer them and avenge them through our own pain. Ultimately we let others hurt us. We attract the boomerang.

Blaming is circular. Blaming is boring. Blaming is endless. If you don't believe me, try the following exercise.

Self-Responsibility Test 4: Blaming

- *Think of all the causes of your unhappiness, and think of all the people who "made" you unhappy.*
- *Now start blaming. Really let yourself go. Blame out loud. Blame as much as you want to. Shout it out loud. Yell and bawl. Don't let anything hold you back.*

I would say "Don't read on until you've finished," but you will never finish. Blaming never comes to an end. If you tried the exercise, my guess is that either you stopped pretty quickly because blaming is not your thing, or you did the exercise for a while, and then stopped out of curiosity to read on. If you did the latter, you surely find yourself in an energy mess right now!

Escape from Blaming Energy

- *Remember how it is to feel happy. Really get into the feeling of happiness. Think of people, things, and experiences that have contributed to your happiness. Now start to praise them out loud. Eulogize! Sing songs of praise. Don't leave yourself out. After all, it was you who let these things make you happy.*
- *Stop when you want to, but don't stop before this exercise in energy maintenance has achieved its goal.*

Blaming is as dangerous as racism. There are groups who are devoted to blaming. Political extremists are such a group: they often take women as their scapegoats. Feminist extremists are another: for some of them it can be dogma that all the problems of the world are due to men. Some psychotherapies blame parents for every problem that children have, as if it were a realistic expectation that ordinary people could become the perfect parents for the perfect child: this results in a modern day witch-hunt with parents designated as witches.

Therapists who are preoccupied with blame are dangerous to their clients. Therapists with unresolved grievances will use their clients to work these out. There have been a number of people recently who made accusations of sexual abuse and then retracted them. Eleanor Goldstein and Kevin Farmer's book *True Stories of False Memories* cites case after case in which therapists of whatever type have imposed these ideas on their clients. They have forced their clients into false memories, without for a moment exploring whether different explanations of and causes for their client's unhappiness were possible.

What kind of people make these accusations of sexual abuse and then recant? The self-designated victims of False Memory Syndrome have one characteristic in common: they are victims of their own tendency to blame. While the persistence that it has taken them to find their own truth cannot be admired enough, their tendency to blame continues. Many blame various books, including Bass and Davis' *The Courage to Heal,* for this epidemic. They also blame the bad practice of therapists and the hysteria of survivor groups. What we get out of any book depends ultimately upon ourselves: we have always to use our discrimination. While Bass and Davis' book does hold some extreme positions, it is for the most part a compassionate book that contains a great deal of wisdom and good advice. It includes a sensible evaluation of the role of psychiatrists and psychotherapists, their practices, and the way survivor groups are conducted which deserves careful attention and which evidently does not receive it from therapists and clients who tend to blame.

If we end up with therapists or in groups that hold extreme views, one way or another it is our choice and we are responsible for it.

Shocking as this may sound, even if you have been seriously abused you cannot put the clock back. All you can do is to respect profoundly your suffering and see to your healing. You will have to use that unpleasant experience to learn from. Awful as it was, you will have to take it on bravely in order to free yourself from its negative effects and get on with building yourself a positive life. It is hard, but it is possible as long as we do not give way to blaming. What I've just said may seem heartless, or insufficiently emotionally involved. That is not what I feel. I have not been raped, but I do know what sexual abuse is. I was tampered with inappropriately as a child and there was no one around I trusted enough to tell about it.

The subject of sexual abuse is so delicate that I want to be clear about the relationship between blaming and respect. When we blame others we do not take responsibility for ourselves. We say, "It is their fault," with the implication that we are helpless and can do nothing about it *now*. It is certainly a fault, and a grave fault, to abuse a child in any way because children are indeed helpless and powerless in the face of abusive adults. People who have abused children probably deserve severe punishments, but I wonder whether they don't also deserve our compassion: such people must be so terrifyingly cut off from Soul energy.

The Tendency to Feel Guilty

To accept responsibility should not be confused with feeling guilty. We all make mistakes. It is part of a normal learning process. When we learn from mistakes they have served their purpose. Until we have learned from them, we will repeat them. They are there to teach us.

Can we be self-responsible without being guilty? Isabelle batters her children. Why? Because she was battered as a child, as were her brothers and sisters. In Isabelle's home, when the children did not comply with the demands of the parents they were beaten. The experiences of our earliest childhood create our idea of what is normal because they were our norm. As Isabelle was battered, it is normal for her to batter her children, and she will continue to do so until, through becoming aware of what she is doing, she asks herself questions and has doubts. Isabelle is innocent because she does not know how to do things in a better way; she is responsible because she is capable of *learning* how to do things in a better way. Certainly if she remembers being battered and how horrible it was for her, she is obliged to seek therapeutical help. It is our responsibility to question our beliefs and behaviors, and always to ask ourselves if we are doing the best possible given the circumstances.

Are we are responsible for creating our ailments? We are certainly responsible for looking after the health of our minds and bodies. By inhaling poisonous smoke, smokers endanger their own lungs, heart, and other organs, as well as endanger those of other people around. People who drink do the same thing, only they put their liver in danger first of all. It would be much better for these people (and would not cost any more!) to undertake their development and to enhance the quality of their lives, rather than to damage their health and to diminish the quality of their lives. These are obvious examples. On the other hand, it makes me sad that people who suffer from serious ailments such as multiple sclerosis and cancer are blamed and made to feel guilty for their illnesses by people with inflexible and accusing attitudes. Life can be stressful. Genetics and the level of planetary pollution play a part. No one is perfect. Compassion and a helping hand seem more appropriate than blame. Some people are able to take responsibility for their illness, to get well or to die serenely and peacefully—one or the other—being advanced in their personal and spiritual development. Others do not have the means to do this, and cannot imagine that they have any responsibility for their health. This adds to their suffering because they have no hope and experience themselves as victims. Every extreme attitude—all fanaticism—is dangerous and unhealthy on every level: mental, emotional, and spiritual.

What about destiny? There is evidence that shows that we are responsible for much that happens in our lives. During a session of self-exploration we may become aware that we chose our parents before our birth in order to learn particular lessons, lessons learned joyfully as well as through suffering. We may also remember decisions made in a previous lifetime that we would come back to learn something in particular or to be with someone in particular.

Feeling guilty is counter-productive. Try the following exercise.

Guilt and Disempowerment

- *Get into the usual comfortable position for inner work. Be aware of your body. How does your skin feel, your head, your neck, your back, your belly? Sense your energy-field.*
- *Now start to think about the things you feel guilty for and the people you feel guilty towards. Do this consciously and observe what happens to your body and to your energy-field. Take no more than five minutes.*

What I expect happened is that your energy-field got smaller and smaller, weaker and weaker, until at the end you felt incapacitated. When we are incapacitated we cannot do anything, so we cannot proceed on our Soul Path.

Here is an empowering way of dealing with guilt.

Guilt and Empowerment

- *Use the Listing Technique with the phrase below:*
  "I feel guilty towards (name of a person) because . . . "

- *Now, taking one person at a time, make a list of all the thoughts that come into your mind and the feelings in your body after the following phrases:*
    "Something I could do to repair the damage is . . . "
- *Take an item on your list and ask yourself whether you are willing or unwilling to repair the damage caused.*
- *If you are willing to repair it, try listing your instant responses after this phrase:*
    "I will repair the damage by . . . "

Sometimes we are unable to repair the damage because a person is dead, out of reach, or will not let us. In these cases, our complete willingness to make reparation is enough.

Feelings of guilt are productive only when they lead us to commit ourselves more deeply to our Soul Quest, to undertake effective therapy so that we do not repeat our harmful behavior, and to make constructive reparation. In the course of our lives we will, almost inevitably, cause pain to others. Part of our learning process and theirs is dealing with this. Our Soul Path task is to acknowledge our responsibility and to take the appropriate steps. It is also to forgive ourself. The task of the people we have hurt is to forgive us: that is their lesson.

> *Refusing to be guided by guilt, shame, and anxiety is a major step towards making room within oneself for reason and love.*
> —Peter Breggin, *Toxic Psychiatry* (p. 278)

And love is Soul.

FOUR
Skillful Values

The Soul Path is paved with Ethics, and at every step our values are tested. Values require choices. Many Soul Quest tests of values concern time and money.

Some people cultivate "spiritual attitudes." Often they take money as their criterion for discriminating between the material and the spiritual. George, on his moral high horse, once told me that money was dirty and evil. These were the ideas he was brought up with. He had no incentive to become rich, and not much incentive to work either! I told him it was immoral to remain poor if he was able to earn money. "You don't have to keep your money for yourself," I said, "You can use it to feed the starving, educate the uneducated, recycle the out-of-work. Nothing forces you to keep the money you earn. You can safely earn vast fortunes of money and keep as little as you like for yourself. What you cannot morally do," I told him, "is deprive others, and that is what you are doing by refusing to earn as much money as possible."

Soul and Money

Money is a highly visible and tangible form of energy: it can be seen and felt, and described in words and numbers. It is an impersonal, neutral, and innocent means for energy exchanges between individuals or countries. *That is really all it is.* What people do with money has nothing to do with objective money. All of our thoughts about money, besides the objective recognition of its usefulness for energy exchanges, are projections. They are our own personal ideas, assimilated from our parents, society, religion, and life-experience.

When I ran my school for personal and spiritual development, I believed it was fair to give everybody who applied a chance to try. The Money Training came halfway through the school year. The Money Training is a way of looking at our relationship with money: what we project onto money, what our parents projected onto money and imposed on us, and what our society projects onto money and imposes on us. It's purpose is to make us conscious of the suffering connected with learned attitudes to, and ideas about, money that have no basis in fact or reality. The Money Training was the most difficult part of the school year—for the students and for me. It was also an infallible way of sorting out students. Those who were not committed to their Soul Quest dropped out before it, sensing that it would test their sincerity beyond its limits. It was much more rare that students dropped out after it, but once one did: she discovered that her money could not buy her out of facing her self. All her life money had been her means for manipulation. On this occasion it did not work. The Money Training increases self-esteem by breaking through illusions. For the "survivors" of the Money Training, the rest of the school year was fun and games.

Because money is so absolutely neutral, it is a clear mirror for projections. That is why quite a few examples in this book concern money. Many people identify money with manipulating or being manipulated. How we relate to money and whether we use it as a means of manipulation or respect it as a means of energy exchange is a demonstration of our self-esteem. That is why money trainings go so deep and are so challenging for both trainers and participants.

Self-esteem is the source of our ability to succeed. It is the strength from which we express our wishes and needs, allow ourselves to be happy, and dare to have new experiences. We expect that others hold us in the same esteem as we hold ourselves: we will not accept less, and we do not very often get more. Often we project our self-esteem, or its absence, into our relationship with money. Money is the battleground upon which the power-games in a family are fought out. Parents control their children by withholding money; adolescents punish their parents by mismanaging their money; adult children control their parents by refusing to earn money and become financially self-responsible. Power-games are always lost on both sides.

In the philosophy of some of the new therapies, people are judged on the quantity of their wealth. Then, having money is a goal in itself and the quantity of money possessed is taken as an indicator of spiritual development and empowerment. Usually people go into money trainings in order to become rich fast. Usually the teacher or trainer considers that s/he is entitled to be tithed to—i.e., that "followers" ought to give him or her one-tenth of their income or wealth—forever. There is exploitation on both sides.

There are always people capable of being happy who, although they have little money, nevertheless always have enough to cover all their needs and more left over to share. There are always unhappy people who, although they have a lot of money, never have enough to be able really to enjoy it, to indulge themselves, to share with their children and families, to be generous with their friends or to support people in need. Everything depends on the way that we look at the world: is our cup half-full or half-empty? Are we worth a half-full cup, or only a half-empty one? With good self-esteem our cup is at least half-full and we are grateful for what is in it.

Sometimes on the Soul Quest we have plenty of money, sometimes just enough, and sometimes what feels like too little. On our Soul Quest we have the opportunity to cope with many different situations.

Victims and Martyrs

If we give our time to our development, we have to leave aside other occupations and interests. If we use our money to pay for our development, we will have less to spend elsewhere. Sometimes we have to choose between amusing ourselves and taking a holiday or making further commitments to our Soul Quest and using our time for workshops and trainings. Sacrifices may be demanded. To sacrifice means to give up something of less value in order to follow a higher objective, and to do that in a spirit of gratitude.

When we give up something we may fall into the attitude of the victim, we may play the martyr, or we may simply decide to take responsibility for our decision and take on the sacrifices required with gratitude that we are able to make them. A victim thinks: "Why should I use my time and my money to put my life in order when it is the fault of my parents, of my school, of my society that I am suffering and do not succeed? I who never have either enough time or enough money." A martyr is always busy blaming others: "I don't have enough time because my children, my parents, my employers need me too much," or "I don't have enough money to buy myself the things I want and to pay for the workshops that lead to development, because I/my husband/my parents don't earn enough." A person capable of making sacrifices takes the position: "These are my values. These are my goals. These are the things that I appreciate and find important for my Soul Quest. I am responsible for achieving them and I can do this in a positive way and with a positive attitude. In order to attain them I will do what is necessary without causing harm to other beings."

Victims and martyrs live on Ego-level. Their attitudes are manipulative. The Soul Quest demands sacrifices. When we move to Soul-level, we decide to give something up in order to attain a higher goal. We exercise our choice. We take the responsibility of directing our lives. We are dignified, responsible, courageous, empowered. Soul-Questing is undertaken in this spirit. To sacrifice is to give its correct importance to what is truly valuable. Every time we take a step forwards, we leave something else behind us. Every day of our lives has its joys and its mournings.

Self-Responsibility Test 5: The victim-martyr test

- *Think of a recent experience when you were faced with a time-and-money choice. Go back to the situation and remember the details. What was the possible purpose? Was the higher choice clear to you? Could you identify in which direction your Soul Path lay, and in which your Ego-path?*
- *How did you make your choice? Like a victim? Like a martyr? Or did you make a sacrifice in all dignity?*

FIVE
Skillful Self-Esteem

Self-esteem is Soul-esteem. Without self-esteem, we do not even begin our Soul Path: we do not feel good enough to do so. Self-esteem is empowering: we believe that we are worthy to transform our lives from Ego-level to Soul-level. In this world that we all share with each other more or less well, good self-esteem leads to good relationships and good relationships to good sharing. Enough self-esteem all round will lead to all humankind living in peace together. This is, surely, the greatest challenge of our shared life here on Earth and the ultimate Soul Quest task.

Self-esteem can be lost before conception. The inner life and well-being of eggs and sperms is affected if potential parents eat unhealthy foods or use harmful drugs.

Self-esteem can be lost in the womb. Babies know if they are desired by their parents, if their gender is pleasing to their parents, and if their parents welcome them and can care for them. Some people have a baby as they might buy a puppy: they want something to amuse them and to love them. Or they want for themselves the experience of bringing up a baby, in the same way that they want the experience of having a dog or cat or goldfish. But what about the experience for the baby? Babies grow up and cannot be given away as puppies so often are when the fantasy becomes reality. Puppies have entitlements to respect and a good home and *children have this right too*. To want to produce a child is the natural biological instinct of the physical body, but this does not give anyone the "right" to have a child. The child's right is that we consider responsibly what kind of a home we offer. Bringing a child thoughtlessly and without self-responsibility into a home that cannot care for it or educate it properly is child-abuse. No one ever has the right to abuse a child.

For most parents and children, birth is the external beginning of disempowerment. Most births still fail to enhance the self-esteem of parents and their babies. It could be different. The work of doctors like Frédérick Leboyer and Michel Odent—who recognize the Soul-level holiness of babies—ought to have led to a more respectful and compassionate birth for every baby, but to the great shame of our Western societies, progress in this domain remains pitiful. Too many babies continue to be born in unholy Ego-level circumstances which are cruel and brutal for them and their parents, in the hospitals of the rich and so-called "civilized" countries.

Very few of us escaped from childhood with our self-esteem undamaged. Very few childhoods are free of hurt and pain. Very few children have modeled for them truly loving relationships or effective communication. As this poem says, children live what they learn:

CHILDREN LIVE WHAT THEY LEARN

by Dorothy Law Holte

If a child lives with criticism
he learns to condemn

If a child lives with hostility
he learns to fight

If a child lives with ridicule
he learns to be shy

If a child lives with shame
he learns to feel guilty

If a child lives with tolerance
he learns to be patient

If a child lives with encouragement
he learns confidence

If a child lives with praise
he learns to appreciate

If a child lives with fairness
he learns justice

If a child lives with security
he learns to have faith

If a child lives with approval
he learns to like himself

If a child lives with acceptance and friendship
he learns to find love in the world.

When a child is hurt, in ways described in the poem or in other ways, unless the wound is healed, it remains an ongoing source of suffering. As the child goes through adolescence to adulthood, its Inner Child—the child it was when it was wounded—continues to live on, hurt and suffering, hidden but influential. Some people are inhabited by many wounded Inner Children, having been hurt at so many different periods during their childhood and adolescence.

Our first relationship lessons take place in our family, taught by our caretakers, consciously and unconsciously. In the first six or seven years of our lives, well before our critical spirit has had the time to develop, we learn relationships in an indirect and subliminal way. From conception we are immersed in the relationship between our parents. We live in it as we live in our childhood home. It becomes inscribed in our heart, mind, body, and spirit. If, by some good fortune, our parents' relationship is loving and has other Soul-level qualities, we, in our turn, have every possibility of constructing a healthy relationship. If, on the other hand, our parents' relationship has been unhappy and limited to Ego-level, we are likely to create something similarly destructive and uninspiring. In relationships, we tend to repeat what we have learned. If our parents are always criticizing and complaining about each other and inviting their children to take sides, or if they are physically violent with each other, we too may do this with our partners. The poem is right.

As children, we observe the relationship that our parents have with their own parents, families, friends, and colleagues, work and society, and these relationships too become our norm. They too inscribe themselves into our behavior patterns and our expectations, and we are unconscious that this programming has taken place. In all innocence and ignorance, we live it out. Our parents bequeath to us their relationship with life, and we inherit it long before they die! If they have bequeathed to us a Soul-level example, we are lucky. If not, it is a Soul Quest task to transform what we have learned.

Communication skills, too, are bequeathed. If our parents' communication was loving, we have had a Soul-level example. If our parents did not know how to communicate, we have not learned the words to express our feelings, desires, joys, and fears. As intimacy is based upon good communication, we have difficulties being intimate.

Communication is speaking and listening. Parents who do not know how to listen to themselves cannot listen to each other or to their children. Children who are not listened to stop listening to themselves. To listen to someone is to recognize that they exist. Good listening creates trust, confidence, and sensitivity, qualities that are essential for good relationships.

What about the influence of past lives on our self-esteem? Past-life work shows that our birth is the pattern of empowerment or disempowerment, self-esteem or self-abuse that we bring with us into this lifetime to learn from. Nevertheless, the concept of past lives *should not be manipulated to justify preventable means of abuse in the present.* There is no need for fatalism. It is our Soul Quest task to make available the best chances possible to all life forms and to the planet. The happier the next generation, the happier the world.

The concept "Inner Child" is a metaphor for our realizable potential and our essential innocence. When the Inner Child is wounded, people either withdraw from the world or become dangerous politicians or dictators. Innocence is a guide to Soul-level living.

Recovering our Inner Child means healing our childhood wounds and bringing the enthusiasm, hope, altruism, and all-round well-being of a healthy child into our adult life and into the world. It is a Soul Quest task to become the ideal parents for our own Inner Child—no one else can do it for us, nor can we do it for anyone else, although we can always be helpful. It is our responsibility to realize our potential. It belongs not only to us, but to the whole world.

SIX

Skillful Awareness: A Process

Awareness is the passageway from Ego to Soul: the more aware Ego is, the better its connection to Soul. Awareness tunes us in to Soul Energy. There are passages on our path when Ego resists Soul. Awareness skills sensitize us to these energy changes and return us to the enjoyment of living on Soul-level. On the Soul Quest awareness does all the work. It is the fundamental factor that of itself induces change. We do not need to worry about how to do things differently. As long as our awareness is good we advance on our Soul Path.

Awareness is a process. The first step is attention: through attention we witness objectively our feelings, thoughts, and actions. The next step is respect: we respect what we observe and do not imagine or fantasize that it is different from what it is. Ego likes excuses and explanations. Ego Therapy ends with them, while Soul Therapy goes beyond them. The third step is acceptance: acceptance is the difference between reality and fantasy. Ego may fear reality. Soul does not. We can only integrate and learn from what we have accepted.

The focus of our awareness is not limited to ourselves. Through awareness we relate our internal world to the external world.

Attention, Respect, and Acceptance are, each in their own right, Soul Therapy Skills.

Skillful Attention

Attention connects us—to our selves, to others, and to the world. When our attention is flowing we live in the present and are conscious of the moment.

Self-responsibility means attending to ourselves: meeting our suffering, doubts, disappointments, fears, anxieties, wishes, and hopes; meeting our joys and sadness, our successes and failures, our behavior patterns, our judgments, our light and shadow. Attending to ourselves is often difficult. It reveals the wounds that we have spent years trying not to feel. If we have been profoundly hurt, connecting to our wounded self is so painful and frightening that our first steps require accompaniment and support. We need to learn how to be close to ourselves safely, and yet the basic skills are those we have been taught not to have. They have been labeled "selfishness."

When we can attend to ourselves we can attend to another person. Attention and intimacy are connected. We can be frightened of that, too. Skills in intimacy are related to skills in attention. To connect is to take down the barriers of self-defense and to trust.

Here is a test that helps us to discover something about our attention:

Attention Test

Part 1. Can you focus your attention on yourself?

- *What happens if you focus your attention on something so simple and so inseparable from yourself that you do it all the time? Take, for example, your breathing. What happens if you just watch your breath enter and leave your body? Don't try to change anything. Don't judge quality, depth, or rhythm. Just observe it for the length of twenty breaths:*
- *Can you observe with awareness the feelings in the various parts of your body and the changes in your emotional state that occur during this period while you use your breath to anchor yourself in awareness and in consciousness, or does your mind wander, fleeing, drawn away into unconsciousness by your thoughts or feelings?*

Part 2. Can you focus your attention on another person?

- *What happens if you give your attention to another person?*
- *If you think of the people you love best in this world, can you let your attention flow out to them from your heart and mind, or do you find yourself erecting barriers against them in the form of judgments, or anger recreated by your memories of old grievances, or in some other way?*
- *Can you focus your attention on another person for the length of twenty breaths?*

Skillful Respect

Respect in the process of awareness is willingness to see things realistically, as they are, and not to impose our attitudes, fantasies, wishes, hopes, and desires upon them.

The basic rule of respect is not to blame and not to make excuses.

At a certain level of development we realize our suffering comes from our character, thoughts, and expectations and that we have some responsibility in creating it. When we know this it is irrelevant to blame others and pointless to make excuses for ourselves. Instead, with compassion for ourselves we understand that we have chosen our suffering in the service of our Soul Path to learn some particular lessons. Moments like this are moments of grace and vision. Their sign is that we use the phrase, "I had to learn. . . ." This way we honor our Soul Quest.

Philip comes from a family of farmers that goes back for many generations. In his adolescence, he had an accident that made it impossible for him to do any hard physical labor and also the sports that he loved. During a Conscious Breathing session he became aware that damaging himself was his only way to change the course of his education. His communication with his parents was difficult and he did not have sufficient confidence in them simply to ask for their support and understanding when he realized he had made a wrong career choice. Now, ten years later he recognizes the benefit of the change that he could make after his accident—

but what a way to arrive at his goal! Philip became aware that on some level he had chosen to have the accident and he respected the deep sadness that came with this discovery. His pattern of not—under any circumstances—expressing his needs was the root of his problems. With this discovery came another one: that it did not have to be this way. Philip realized that he did not have to hurt himself to get what he needed. He began to express himself in better ways and to make others aware of his needs.

Respect in life is visionary, enabling, and ennobling. In Soul-Questing, we respect that all human beings are on a Soul Path, whether they are conscious of it or not. We respect the equality of all human beings and their right to be as they are and where they are on their Soul Path.

Skillful Acceptance

Acceptance means saying "Yes." Acceptance means observing *without trying to change.* We are aware only to the extent that we accept. Acceptance has nothing to do with submission. That is playing the role of victim.

Sometimes acceptance is almost banal. I was giving a Conscious Breathing session to Geraldine. Her head was turned away from me. I simply acknowledged its position, saying, "I notice that your head is turned away from me." Geraldine used that whole session to explore her tendency to turn away, with powerful results. The best therapists I have ever worked with have, through their acceptance, simply given me back to myself. I do not know of anything more valuable.

Acceptance means observing without judging. Discernment is always appropriate. When we judge we criticize destructively and reject. Judging involves us in "oughts" and "shoulds" rather than in exploring what is actually happening. Here's an example. Lesley came for a session. Tears came and she fought them back. Her judgment was that she had already cried for far too long over what was hurting her, so she rejected her grief. But Lesley was an abused child and had a lot to cry over. Her grief was real and it was still there. With some effort she was persuaded to let her tears flow and to accept them. This brought insights that she could integrate. Several similar sessions progressively diminished her grief.

Here is an acceptance exercise:

Acceptance through Awareness of Breathing

• *Put your attention on your breathing and observe the breath entering and leaving your body without trying to change anything. Just observe the breath as it is. It may be long or short, deep or shallow, fast or slow, comfortable or uncomfortable, free-flowing or tight and blocked. It may be mainly in the chest or in the abdomen or it may fill both. Do not judge whether you are breathing "correctly" or not—in any case, how can you know? Different breathing is right in different circumstances. Just witness your breathing.*
• *Could you just accept your breathing as it was or did you have any number of ideas about how it should be? Were you accepting or judging and evaluating?*

Acceptance means living in reality rather than in ideals, fantasies and projections, and having our wishes and our dreams cloud over our view. If we accept that we are unhappy, we enter the path that leads us through that unhappiness and out of it. If we do not accept and acknowledge what we have to feel grateful for, we cut ourselves off from our joy, from God, or Soul, or the Self, or that aspect of Energy that is the Highest—whichever name we give to it.

Awareness and Conditioning

Through awareness we escape from our conditioning. Without any training in Soul Therapy skills, unconsciously we cling to the familiar. We cling to our parents and to what we expect of them; to our spouse, children, family, home-town, country, and world. We cling to our ideas, opinions, beliefs, desires and habits, our character and tendencies. We cling to our "we musts" and "I shoulds," our grievances and our excuses.

A woman in her late fifties or early sixties called Dora came to see me. Dora wished to join the school, but not this year because she had already used up all her holidays. And there was the problem of her partner, who would certainly be cross with her if she did not spend all her week-ends and holidays with him. And she was unable to make decisions because her parents had always made her decisions for her. And one should not under any circumstances forget the serious problem of her character. A long recitation followed of all the things that a committee of astrologers had said about her. Dora, who had done years of psychotherapy of many different kinds, had learned to explain herself and to excuse herself. She had learned to produce reasons that proved she was not responsible for herself and that maneuvered someone else into that position. She was the prisoner of her much-studied character. I explained to her that we inherit our character and also the means to go beyond its limitations, and that we can use our self-knowledge to go beyond our habits. Dora had mastered Ego Therapy. She had learned to describe herself and she clung to the rigid and unchangeable boundaries of her descriptions. She had not yet learned the awareness that would enable her to separate from her explanations and really develop.

Awareness makes detachment possible. It is the way out, the door upon whose threshold we can leave the habits that lead to failure. Peter had a strong tendency to criticize himself negatively, no matter what he did. He was especially convinced that he expressed himself badly. We explored this judgment, working to discover in which circumstances he expressed himself badly and when he expressed himself to his satisfaction. Moving from generalization to realistic appraisal, Peter discovered that he expressed himself badly in front of people who abused their authority, as his father had done in his childhood. Otherwise, there were many situations where he could express himself adequately or even well. As Peter became aware, he became free. His destructive thoughts became like old clothes that no longer fit as he developed the skill to discern their relationship with reality.

Peter began to use this tendency as a source of information. When he decided to change his job, he carefully chose an employer to whom he could express himself.

Through awareness comes realism.

SEVEN
Skillful Gratitude

Greed is Ego; Gratitude is Soul. Gratitude lifts us from Ego-level to Soul-level.

Gratitude is unfashionable in a consumer society whose cup is always half-empty and that thinks in terms of what it does not yet have, rather than rejoicing in what it already has. Gratitude says that our cup is already more than half-full and still filling up. It says, "Thank you."

Gratitude opens up the energy-field and makes receiving possible. Try this exercise:

Gratitude Energy

Part 1

- *Think of all the things you want and that you do not yet have. Make a list of them. Just let the list of all of your unfulfilled desires flow.*
- *How do you feel?*

Part 2

- *Now make a list of all the things you have to be grateful for.*
- *Now how do you feel?*
- *Which good energies does gratitude generate for you?*

Often clients come pushed to Soul-Questing by suffering and despair. They cannot see any good in themselves. They see only failures and no successes. I have a lot of compassion for this real and painful state of suffering. Nevertheless, if I leave a person in that state they lose the strength that remains to them. So I give them this gratitude exercise to lift them from Ego-level to Soul-level.

The Gratitude Exercise

• *List two hundred of your good points, your assets, what you have.*

I give this exercise at the end of a session, at the door, casually, while saying goodbye. The client will look at me with disbelief, wide-eyed, mouth open. Impossible. I nod my head, and with an expression of complete innocence—I'm a specialist in this expression, as my clients and students can witness—I say, "Yes. Your first two hundred assets. It's easy to do. And when you've done that you can start on the list of your next two hundred." And I smile, and shut the door.

How did you feel when you read the exercise? Did the very idea get on your nerves, or did you do it? Were you immediately inspired? Did you feel your energy change?

Clients arrive for the next session full of apologies and excuses. They explain that they could only list six, or sixteen, or twenty-six assets that they are certain they have. I am satisfied. The exercise has succeeded. However difficult and painful the situation, clients have recognized that they have at least some personal resources. But I don't say this. I say, "Look at your body. Your head functions: you have two eyes, two ears, you can see and hear, you can speak and express yourself; your hands function: each finger can bend even in *two* places, your organs . . . ," and I send the client back to complete the list of two hundred assets . . . and the second list.

It is not obvious or to be taken for granted that any part of our body functions as it should: it is a daily reason for gratitude. The more we recognize our competence on all levels, the more strength we have to confront obstacles and to advance.

To be grateful is to recognize the quality of our life. We are often so self-critical that we forget to recognize our achievements and our successes. It is the same with regard to our society: we are often so critical that we do not see its achievements and feel grateful for them. Soul Quest skills have an application in every aspect of life, including politics and the economy. It is important to be discerning, and indeed we are obliged to be critical so that the necessary changes and improvements can take place. But our criticism must be fair and well-founded, an honest and constructive criticism that respects and enhances what there is to be grateful for, and builds upon it.

Being grateful opens the heart. What we are grateful for has value for us and we look after it. When we are grateful for our successes and those of our society, we wish to share and improve the lives of others in every way we can.

EIGHT
Skillful Humility

Skillful humility prevents us from turning our Soul Quest into an Ego trip.

On our Soul Quest capacities often considered to be extraordinary or transpersonal spontaneously become ours. They are gifts. They come, as naturally as branches grow on trees and flowers grow on plants. Skillful Humility enables us to stay modest and ordinary in all circumstances, to learn and to serve. Through Skillful Humility we *never* think that we are better than anyone else, no matter what our gifts may be. Humility has nothing to do with humiliation, which is a way of abusing oneself and others.

The opposite of humility is arrogance, pretentiousness, delusion, power-games, and all types of spiritual materialism. This appropriate expression comes from the title of a book, *Cutting through Spiritual Materialism,* by Chögyam Trungpa, and this is his explanation and definition:

> *Walking the spiritual path properly is a very subtle process; it is not something to jump into naively. There are numerous sidetracks which lead to a distorted, ego-centered version of spirituality; we can deceive ourselves into thinking we are developing spiritually when instead we are strengthening our egocentricity through spiritual techniques. This fundamental distortion may be referred to as* spiritual materialism. —(*back cover, 1973 edition*)

74

There is a vast difference between Ego-Questing and Soul-Questing. Some people undertake their development, calling it spiritual, in order to impress their friends. Some belong to a group whose rule is "the more one does, the more one belongs," and whose members must try every new method. Some do one or two short trainings or buy a title, and offer themselves as group leader or "master." There are people who become the devotees of a guru and boast about "their" guru's purported powers. They appropriate the guru to themselves as if s/he were a material object that they owned, and use "their" guru's purported powers and wisdom to boost their own self-esteem.

Some people suddenly have a dramatic and impressive experience, with no foundation of knowledge into which to integrate it, and immediately present themselves as gurus on that basis. Some people seek to develop for the power that they believe they will gain over others: the kind of power that works so that the more they have, the less others have—less space, less respect, fewer rights. Real empowerment has this quality: *the more I am empowered, the more others are empowered.* The humble sharing of power is the essence of the Soul Quest. Through the present worrisome state of our planet, we are all learning that it is through skillful sharing that we will have a better, safer world.

NINE
Skillful Simplicity

I read somewhere that the Buddha said, "Everything is simple. That is why nobody understands it." I do not think this quotation is authentic. Nevertheless, it is a lovely idea and expresses a fundamental truth.

On our Soul Quest we learn many things that are exciting and inspiring. At last we re-experience capacities which we remember having as children, but which became diminished or lost to us over the years: instinct, intuition, clairvoyance, vision, joy, unconditional love. When we rediscover these abilities, we have many emotions: the joy of having re-found them mixed with the resentment of having been cut off from them; pride in our abilities and the urge to compare and compete: we wonder whether we have more or less of these abilities than others. We are shaken up, and have more than ever the need to be simple.

The Soul Quest is essentially simple. It only requires giving up everything that does not belong to it. When we are simple, we begin to *know* because nothing stops us from knowing: not pride, nor spiritual materialism, nor resentment, nor confusion, nor thoughts about the past or the future, nor theories. We live in the present and Soul energy flows. We do what we have to do and our destiny accomplishes itself effortlessly through us. Everything is harmonious and peaceful—at last.

When I began to work as a therapist, a friend with a lot of perception sent me a postcard on which just the word SIMPLIC-ITY was printed. I was so far from simplicity at the time that I did not speak to her for a year. But I kept the card. After a year, I stuck it on the wall of the room where I work to remind me. It is still there.

I once had a student called Edith who imagined that I knew a great deal, and who attributed to me—with a conviction that came from I don't know where—enormous wisdom. Edith was very impressed with this wisdom she imagined that I possessed. One day I said to her, "Edith, I will tell you the truth. I know only two things." Edith waited with baited breath: what would these two great pearls of wisdom be? She prepared herself to remember them forever. "Only two things," I repeated in a serious voice, "One is that the world is round, and the other, . . . " I pulled faces, scratched my head, and looked disappointed, "The other is. . . . Oh dear. I've forgotten." Edith burst out laughing.

I like to make people laugh. And what is more simple and healing than laughter?

TEN

Skillful Trust, Faith, and Surrender

First we trust, then we take the blind leap of faith, and then, as we fall or fly, we surrender. Trust, faith, and surrender are a process!

Before we embark seriously upon our Soul Quest we cannot imagine what it involves. In my school, at the end of the first year, which has been joyful, exciting, and satisfying but also very testing, all the students would say, "I never imagined that I would go through so much. I never imagined that I would learn so much. Oh, là là!" And they would say the same again at the end of the second year. By the third and fourth year they knew what was coming!

Why? What do we come across when we commit ourselves to this path? We come across *ourselves*. We find ourselves confronted with our own character: our habits, our patterns of thought, speech, and behavior, our values—with everything that we identify as being "me." But this "me" is the learned "me." It is the way of experiencing, describing, and explaining ourselves that we have acquired.

The learned "me" is known and familiar. It contains no surprises. It is responsible as much for our successes as it is for those aspects of our personality that perturb us and cause us to fail. We learn what our real self is through the surrender of our learned self. We let it go.

Soul-Questing means to surrender everything that we identify with. Our trust and faith are tested when we let go. We trust enough to take the risk of losing everything in the hope of finding everything: of discovering what is truest and most valuable and really belongs to us.

Ego loves the familiar. Often we are afraid of letting go. We are afraid to give up doing things in the way that we have always done them and reacting to circumstances in the way we have always reacted. We are afraid of finding ourselves helpless and unprotected. To some extent our fear is well-founded. When we have truly surrendered and left behind us an old way of functioning, a moment or a period of uncertainty follows. Our old behavior patterns no longer fit, like outgrown clothes. They no longer function, like rusty machinery. Our habitual responses no longer drive us and there is a gap in which we do not know what to do. This space does not remain empty for long. We invent better ways of functioning and the richness of the new possibilities feels miraculous. For the first time in our lives we are able to *choose* how to be. In letting go, we leave behind what has been imposed upon us and take up the way which is authentically ours. We consciously develop. We consciously use our imagination and our creativity in order to manage situations better, to express and to assert ourselves better, to create better relationships, to take our place in the world better, to succeed better. We move closer to Soul-level. Letting go has positive results.

The opposite of letting go is holding on, mistrust, the wrong amount of doubt, fear of change, Ego-level.

The process of abandoning old behaviors and discovering better ones takes place regularly on the Soul Path. It can be, but it is not always, dramatic. Here is a "letting go" exercise.

Letting Go

- *Be daring enough to leave behind you as you get up one morning all your old baggage of ideas, thoughts, knowledge, convictions, certainties, attitudes, beliefs, and the rest. Be willing to leave your bed not knowing anything, not believing anything, not holding on to anything.*
- *Observe what comes back during the day, and check with yourself regarding every thought, every idea, every conviction, etc., "Is this really mine or is this just a habit? Does this really belong to me? Do I really want to keep it?"*
- *Your answer will be "Yes," for what is valuable. The rest can well be let go.*

Soul has no attitudes or vested interests except in Ethics. This exercise frees energy and creativity. Do it regularly.

ELEVEN
Skillful Loving

Love is the basis of the Soul Quest, of spiritual life, and of all development. Soul is Love. No matter by which terminology Soul is described, and no matter by which religion or philosophy, Soul is Love. If it is not Love, it is not Soul.

Somebody asked me, "What is love?" A theoretical answer is too difficult. In general it is what stops people from harming each other and the planet, and moves them in the direction of ethical behavior and the Soul Quest. We can feel what love is more easily than we can talk about it. On an energy level, love is connected with the heart. Here is an exercise in loving:

Open Your Heart

- *Think of someone who has annoyed you today through the little kind of annoyances of everyday life: your partner did not clean the dishes, your children had to be hassled to do their homework, a traffic warden gave you a ticket. . . . The ordinary, boring, repetitive annoyances of everyday life.*
- *What feelings do you have? Write them down.*
- *Now bring that person into your mind. Imagine or remember what they look like. Open your heart to them. Stop blaming. Stop feeling angry. Give up all ideas of revenge. Let awareness of their lives, their feelings, their problems, their suffering, their helplessness, and their vulnerability come to you.*
- *Now what feelings do you have? Write them down.*

Sadly, some people do not know how to open their hearts at will. Sadly, I cannot tell you that mine is open all of the time—but I like to think that it is most of the time! If you need to open your heart, here is an exercise:

Being in Your Heart

Part 1

• *Check how you feel. Is your mind peaceful or are your thoughts chaotic? Does your body feel heavy or light? In which area of your body do you have the most feelings: your head? Your neck? Your chest? Your belly? Your legs? Which part precisely do you feel the most at this moment?*

Part 2

• *Now remember a pet you had in your childhood, or a favorite stuffed animal, or some other cherished object. Remember how you loved to feel it, to stroke it. Remember the comfort it brought you. Remember how it felt in your arms when you held it to your heart.*
• *Now how do you feel? Which area of your body do you feel the most now?*

Most usually in this exercise our attention and energy are drawn to an area in the chest between the breasts, at heart level or slightly higher. This is where the heart chakra (which I say more about in Chapter 13) is found. Through this exercise it opens, the area feels warmer and more energized, and we feel more sensitive and compassionate.

Opening our heart chakra prevents pettiness and misunderstanding from taking hold of us. We see the world differently when it is open. Practice opening yours until you can do this at will.

Commitment to the Soul Quest is an act of love. To commit ourselves is to put our energy fully into our effort without thinking "but . . . " or "if . . ." or "perhaps . . ." or "just so long as it does not disturb my life too much."

On our Soul Quest we encounter difficult steps that we have to take and challenging obstacles that we have to surmount. At these times, the limits we impose upon ourselves will block or impede our progress. Our commitment generates the energy necessary to take us beyond our limits. There is a saying that we are born alone and we die alone. I am not as pessimistic as that. There are helpful people everywhere and helpful energies around everyone waiting to be called upon: sometimes we just do not see or sense them well enough. Wonderful friends, teachers, and energies support our Soul Quest.

Soul-Questing is a loving action. Our development serves the development of the people around us through the energy changes in ourselves. It is from the love that we have for ourselves, others, society, and the environment that comes the courage and commitment to embark upon our Soul Quest—our demanding task which takes so much effort and is so inspiring and often so difficult. It is love for the other, as much as for ourselves, which gives us the force to go beyond our tendency to find excuses and to put off until tomorrow our need to change the behaviors that hurt us and others today.

Julian began to work on his development, without telling his wife. Very soon he began to notice that his wife confided in him more, that she became more intimate with him and more open. This led to an improvement in their relationship in general and also in their sex life. As Julian progressed, he noticed that his children approached him more easily and took him increasingly into their confidence. He noticed that at work it became easier for him to collaborate with his colleagues. He became able to take up his place and express his ideas, and he noticed that in doing that he created a space for his colleagues to do the same. Instinctively attracted by the energy that Julian increasingly emanated through his growing awareness and wisdom, and also by the confidence that such energy creates, his colleagues came to consult him and to ask his advice—something that rarely happened before. All this was just through the effect of his development.

Marianne, a secretary, had a very difficult employer. He behaved like a spoiled child—rude, disrespectful, impatient, invasive. She suffered so much that, finding no other solution, she turned to her personal and spiritual development. It must be admitted that it was only after two years of intensive work that the behavior of her boss changed—at least in her direction. He became respectful, appreciative, admiring, and friendly towards her. Marianne has black sparkling eyes and a delightful, gurgling, chuckling laugh. She likes to tell about how two people who irritated each other and made each other nervous have become friends, mutually caring and considerate. And all this happened only because Marianne's energy changed. Her relationship with her husband improved too, as did many other aspects of her life. Her employer, however, only changed in his relationship with Marianne. Unfortunately, he continues to be the same selfish husband and father, and overbearing employer to his other employees.

Sometimes, in the 1970s and 1980s, people who followed the Soul Quest and worked on their personal and spiritual development were accused of egoism or selfishness. They were blamed for only thinking of themselves. But now their contribution to the world is recognized in domains as different as the business world (more and more of the large enterprises offer seminars in personal development to their employees at every level), science (David Bohm, Rupert Sheldrake), psychology (C. G. Jung, Ken Wilber, Hal and Sidra Stone, Stanislav Grof), medicine (Bernie Siegel), the quality of life (Shakti Gawain, Scott Peck), and the quality of death (Elizabeth Kübler-Ross, Stephen Levine), to name only the first few examples that come to mind. There is ever more proof that the people who apply themselves to their Soul Quest benefit the whole world and contribute to its development—which is what Jung said a long time ago. We can draw only one conclusion now, which is that *not to apply ourselves to our development* is the real selfishness.

Love tells us that we have the right as well as the responsibility to discover who we are, the purpose of our lives, and the unique gift that we have to offer the world. As we accomplish each new step and achieve ever more empowerment, it is love that prevents us from abusing it.

Unconditional Love

"How do we learn to love?" someone asked me. Being loving cannot be taught as a sport or a foreign language is taught. We develop our ability to love by removing the obstacles that impede us from loving, through following our Soul Quest. When we work on our process of development, we go beyond the dark and heavy energies, those unhealed scars of our personal pain and suffering, that keep us from loving. We go beyond fear and anger and other feelings that divide us from our fellow beings. Gradually we develop unconditional commitment. We become able to live in compassion for all humankind and their problems. When we can really do that, we have discovered unconditional love. Not before.

Loving the World

Through love, we can go a little further. We can learn to open the door to Soul-Questing for others—in our families, schools, societies; the business, medical, and political worlds—so that the idea of following our Soul Path and committing ourselves to our personal development, and the concept of living fully in harmony with others and the planet, eventually become the norm, and the energy-field of our whole planet becomes pure love.

TWELVE
Body Skills

We act in the world by means of our body. It is the vehicle through which we accomplish our destiny here on Earth.

We are not "only" our body: we inhabit our body. Our body is biological. It has its own path of development, from conception, through gestation, birth, youth, the beginning of sexuality and fertility, the creation of children, the end of fertility, the end of sexuality, and the end of life which is death.

Our body is precious and needs to be looked after.

The Authority of the Body

Our bodies transmit and receive energy. We communicate through body language at least as much as if not more than through words. Our posture and the way we move communicates through space what we feel and think. This is how we attract each other across the crowded room on some enchanted evenings. That is also how we keep each other away, with a "don't come near me" body position.

We cannot overestimate the knowledge and wisdom of our body. Because we can transmit and receive information through it, our body helps us to understand others. It is the *authority* on our self and on other people. When we are with someone whose energy is clear and wholesome, we feel this in our body:

it is relaxed and receptive and we feel happy and confident. When we are in the presence of someone dishonest and unpleasant whose energy is dirty and heavy, we feel it, too, in our body which then feels uncomfortable, ill at ease, tense, defended, tired, or heavy. Our instinct may tell us to fight or to flee. The "fleeing" may manifest as boredom or sleepiness and the "fighting" as irritation or agitation. Our bodies have intelligent reactions.

Tune In to Your Body

Part 1

- *Think of someone you met today or recently that you like a lot.*
- *How does your body feel? Be aware of areas like your neck, shoulders, belly, hands, calves. Do they feel relaxed or tense, light or heavy, supple or stiff?*

Part 2

- *Think of someone you met today or recently that you do not like much.*
- *Now how does your body feel? Be aware again of areas like your neck, shoulders, belly, hands, calves. Do they feel relaxed or tense, light or heavy, supple or stiff?*

Part 3

- *Now go back to thinking about someone you like and repeat Part 1 for skillful energy maintenance.*

Our body is the authority on our physical and mental safety. It knows which places are not good for us: which houses, which shops, which office buildings. Sometimes it knows we should not walk in a certain direction or take a certain airplane, train, or bus. Afterwards, quite often we have no proof that we were acting logically in following our instincts, but sometimes there is a sudden proof: the bus we did not take broke down or crashed; the route we did not follow had long traffic jams; we discover that the friend we did not visit was behaving disloyally.

Sometimes our body knows we should take a particular path, and we have surprising and wonderful meetings.

Our body is our wise and kind teacher. When we take time to listen to its messages, we know whether we are on an Ego-path or a Soul Path. The body feels good on the Soul Path: light, balanced, and harmonious. The body does not feel good on the Ego-path: it feels heavily laden and rigid and struggles to keep itself healthy, supple, and upright. As our body is comfortable on the Soul Path and uncomfortable on the Ego-path, it informs us which path we are on.

Every experience that we have ever had, whether it was pleasant or painful, joyful or sad, is recorded in our body. The memories of each day of our lives are there. Traumas that we have not yet integrated and sorrows that we have not yet expressed are repressed and held there, causing stress and discomfort. For its own health, our body needs us to listen to it and alleviate its burden. Our body needs us to follow the Soul Quest, for its health and well-being.

Our body is the tool of our *inner shaman*. As we receive Soul Quest gifts, we become able to use our body to channel energy, as in massage or healing, each of us according to our gifts. On the Soul Quest we tune in to our body's wisdom and apply it.

Skillful Incarnation

Many religions are ambivalent about the body. They recognize that incarnation on the human plane is essential for following a Soul Quest, and then they devote the whole incarnation to the task of subduing the body. If we hate our bodies we disempower ourselves. I prefer to see the body as something holy, and I think that this is a healthy and growing tendency of our time. Many of the best new therapies use the wisdom of the body for Soul-Questing. It is an integral part of the Soul Quest to enhance our relationship with our body—not through over-exercising or over-dieting or becoming obsessed with it—but through discovering its inherent holiness.

Many people have difficulty in accepting incarnation. They fear and mistrust it. They do not see its spirituality, imagining that spirituality is found anywhere else but in the human body. These people live their humanness in a limited way on an Ego-level. When we accept this extraordinary music, the complex and magnificent fugue that is our humanness, we appreciate and marvel, humble and awed before a holy experience. Let us remember that all the great masters who have shown the path—Moses and the other Jewish prophets, Christ, Mohammed, Confucius, the Buddha, and all of the others—incarnated as human beings.

Grounding

We have a body and tend to identify ourselves with it, but how incarnated are we? How present in our body? Are we in contact with it all of the time, only some of the time, or almost never? Are we willing to incarnate?

For many people it is not at all obvious to take their place in their body because this means accepting that they have been born and confronting life. It is difficult for them to accept their human condition: birth and death, joy and sorrow, success and failure. This problem is expressed in reactions like:

- *"I don't want to be here" (meaning "on Earth").*
- *"I don't want to be in my body."*
- *"I don't want to have a body."*
- *"I never wanted to be born."*
- *"I don't belong to this world."*

Incarnation is achieved through grounding. As human beings we walk upright. Physically we have our feet on the ground and our heads towards heaven. We belong both to Earth and heaven. Symbolically and energetically we link them as they themselves connect through us. To be grounded is to feel the energy of this connection flowing in us and through us, and to draw stability, support, and strength from it. When we are not grounded we simply are not "here": we are not aware and we do not occupy our bodies. We are blown around like leaves in the wind, unable to control our thoughts, feelings, and emotions. We cannot direct our lives. We re-act rather than choose our actions. Just as the reliability with which a building remains standing in favorable and adverse conditions depends on the quality of its foundations, so our empowerment through favorable and adverse conditions depends on our grounding skills. Without good grounding we cannot integrate our experiences on the path of development.

Good grounding enables us to walk on the Earth with confidence, knowing that we belong here. It gives us autonomy: we have no need to impress and nothing to prove. It gives us authority: we are appreciated, consulted, and listened to. We are convincing: we succeed in a job that pleases us. In the family, relationships are harmonious. When we are grounded, we do not get involved in manipulation and power-games. The energy-field that surrounds us radiates empowerment: we place our trust wisely, and people trust us. In our work of development we choose techniques and practitioners well. We advance in a solid way: we do not do too much and we do not chase after sensations or drama. We follow our Soul Quest well.

Without grounding there is no base upon which to construct our Soul Path, nowhere to place our strong and meaningful experiences. We become confused and unsettled. Grounding is our basic discipline.

Grounding is practiced in the same way as a sport: through training. As we are always trying to improve our technique and our skills in the sports that we do, so we should be doing the same with our grounding techniques and skills.

Here are some exercises, presented in order of difficulty and of subtlety. The first are the easiest and the most concrete. The strength of the first two lies in the fact that they are amusing. Have fun!

Bouncing

- *Probably, at this moment you are sitting as you read this book and, as you are reading, it is unlikely that you are feeling much of what is happening in your body. This is exactly how things should be, because you need to be "in your head" in order to read.*
- *Now begin to bounce gently on your buttocks until you can feel them very well. After a moment you will feel very present in your body and in the world. You will feel your buttocks and your legs and feet and you will have a very good contact with your body. You will see your environment very clearly.*
- *Welcome! You are grounded!*

This exercise is amusing and its effect is rapid. Once it has been understood, I can remind a group of it through making a gentle bounce: everyone understands, grounds themselves, and becomes calm, concentrated, present, and attentive.

Carrot Consciousness

- *Imagine fully that you are a carrot. Feel your strong root firmly lodged in the Earth. Feel your red-orange color. Feel your leaves gently moving in the breeze. Feel the strength with which your root pushes itself into the Earth and holds it.*
- *Carrots are amazingly well grounded!*

This exercise too is fun. I use it mostly with people who have great difficulties in grounding. Its results are immediate. I have barely pronounced the instructions before they find themselves truly present. Often it is for the first time in their lives. Then they burst into laughter with wonder and amazement.

Tree-Consciousness 1: Be a Tree

- *Imagine that you are a tree. Feel your roots, which enter deeply into the Earth. Feel the welcome of the Earth and its capacity to nourish.*
- *Feel the spiritual nature of the Earth.*
- *Welcome to the Earth!*
- *What kind of tree are you?*

This exercise helps people to establish a strong connection with the Earth and with their ability to be here. For many it is the first time they experience the spirituality of the Earth, and it is a revelation. They are surprised and moved. When people have no contact with the spirituality of the Earth, they suffer from the delusion that the Earth is not as good as the heavens. They think they are above the Earth and indeed they are, uncomfortably so, as they are not grounded.

To identify with a tree is to discover which kind of a tree we are. Often this leads to the recognition of our empowerment. To imagine that we are a tree is to offer ourselves psychic protection. Try it if you have difficult tasks to perform or a difficult job or if you have to be in the company of difficult people.

If you are finding it very difficult to feel grounded, try drawing or painting a tree. Here is the exercise.

Tree-Consciousness 2: Draw a Tree

- *Draw or paint a tree. Take a large sheet of paper. Give yourself space.*
- *Make the roots very strong. Really show how they support the tree on the Earth and anchor it in it.*
- *Make a strong, straight, healthy trunk.*
- *Make branches that reach outwards into the air and upwards into the sky.*

When we draw or paint a tree, the roots are our physical feet and show the way we relate to the Earth on the energy level. They show whether we are strongly grounded and take our place firmly upon the Earth, or whether we float above it. The trunk is our body, our way of supporting our life. It represents our confidence and our competence in our world. The branches and leaves that go towards the sides show our relationship towards other people and society, and the branches that go upwards show our relationship to the imaginary, the creative, the inventive, and to God or the Highest Principle and our spiritual life.

In meetings or gatherings where the energy is not grounded, it is stabilizing to doodle trees with good roots, strong straight trunks, and branches to the sides and upwards.

The Golden Chain

- *Imagine that a fine chain of gold, very strong and quite unbreakable, comes from the base of your spine and enters the Earth. The chain penetrates right to the center of the Earth, where it finds an immense tree trunk. It turns itself around this tree trunk several times.*

These grounding exercises should be practiced regularly. They are especially useful whenever difficult circumstances have to be faced.

Incarnation Exercise

- *Imagine that a root comes from the base of your spine, like an animal's tail. This root enters the Earth. It connects you with the Earth. Through it, you feel the texture of the Earth and its humidity.*
- *When you feel this contact strongly, begin to draw your in-breath from the Earth, and let your out-breath fall into the Earth. Feel the spirituality of the Earth. Draw strength from the Earth in this way, accepting fully your connection with it.*

Soul and Body

The more we are willing to be here, the more fun we have in life in all of its aspects: relationships, communication, working, creating, giving, receiving, feeling, loving, wholeness, and holiness. When we reject our body, we deny that we exist. We reject the Earth. Rejecting our body is also a way of rejecting God—or whatever name or concept we place upon the Highest that we can conceive of. I'm quite fond of the word "God." It is short and simple.

Most people relate to God on Ego-level. It is a power-game relationship. They incarnate only under certain conditions and it is they who will tell God what these conditions are. They try to

control what they imagine God is through rituals, deals and con-
tracts, and superstitious thought. They think, "God will give me
what *I* want because I have done such-and-such."

For people on Ego-level, God is the father or the mother who
they have never succeeded in controlling. God is the parent who
has disempowered them. They cannot simply trust God. They
negotiate and trade: "If I do that for You, You will do this for
me." They believe in the same way that they buy medical insurance—and the illness that they are buying insurance against is
their life. The unconditional love they demand of God is more
like unconditional obedience and it is not part of what they offer
Him: they do not offer unconditional faith.

Some people relate to God on Soul-level. They incarnate without conditions and say, "Thy will be done," and they mean it.
This is surrender to Soul.

Exercise to Connect Heaven and Earth

• *Stand comfortably or sit on a chair with your feet firmly on the
ground. Feel the contact between your feet and the surface beneath
them and become aware that this surface rests upon the Earth. Draw
your in-breath from the Earth, let your out-breath fall into the
Earth. Feel the spirituality of the Earth. Draw strength from the
Earth in this way. Breathe this way for a while, accepting fully and
respectfully your spiritual connection with the Earth.*

• *Now draw your in-breath from the Earth. Draw it up above your
head, into Heaven, so that you connect Earth and Heaven with your
in-breath, and then let the breath gently fall down through you to
find the Earth again, so that you can join Heaven and Earth with
your out-breath.*

• *Let Earth energy and Heaven energy flow through you. Sense Soul.
Enjoy yourself!*

THIRTEEN
Skillful Energy Hygiene

We are energy-beings. As we progress in our Soul Quest and our awareness expands, we become increasingly aware of this. We discover that we relate not only to the physical world of tangible matter but also to the vast universe of subtle vibrations.

The Subtle Body

We have a physical body, various energy bodies, and different energy centers. Each of these has its own type of energy. The *chakras* are energy centers in the aura. There are many of them. Various systems of chakras are described in classical Indian texts. Acupuncture and reflexology points are also energy centers.

Our subtle energy may express itself through our physical body. Sometimes when we see a person or when we think about them, we have a strong physical reaction which may be positive or negative: our heart may feel open and joyful, or it may ache painfully; our throat may feel blocked and tense. Our body has not been touched: our subtle energies are affected, communicating through our physical body.

The Aura

Our aura is the energy-field that surrounds our physical body. Our physical body has its own particular set of functions and our aura or subtle body has its own separate set. It is just as important to be able to feel our energy body as it is to be able to feel our physical body. The aura has layers or levels which are energy envelopes. The etheric body closely surrounds the physical body and is about a centimeter deep. The next level is the emotional body, whose name describes the nature of its energy and its content. The next energy envelope is the mental body, and then come other levels of subtle energy that connect us to ever more refined and spiritual energies which we become conscious of as we develop. Our aura differs in size according to how we feel: larger when we feel good, smaller when we feel less good. Auras differ in quality according to a person's development in Soul-Questing. The more a person lives their life on Soul-level, the clearer their aura.

The Soul Quest is not always serious. When we have learned how to sense our aura, we can play games with it, as if it were a balloon, making it bigger and smaller. We can take people into it and—when we need to—push people out of it.

The Chakras

The *chakras* are energy centers. The system that most people are familiar with is that of seven chakras:

1. *the root chakra, situated in the region of the perineum*
2. *the sex chakra, situated at the level of the pubic bone*
3. *the solar plexus chakra, situated a little above the navel*
4. *the heart chakra, situated at the level of the heart*
5. *the throat chakra, situated at the level of the throat*
6. *the third-eye chakra, situated between the eyebrows*
7. *the crown chakra, situated above the top of the head.*

We can feel these chakras physically with our hands as areas of warmth or greater concentration of energy a few centimeters above the appropriate location in the physical body.

No chakra is "better" or more valuable than any other. This is Ego-level thinking. The chakras are an energy system and, like any other system, all of the parts need to function well and to be in balance and harmony, otherwise the system does not work.

We are connected to the Earth and grounded through the first chakra, often called the root chakra. If this connection is inadequate, we are like a house without foundations or a tree without roots: we do not remain upright in difficult situations and we cannot resist storms. Self-responsibility begins in this energy center. The second chakra, the sex chakra, is the source of our creativity, whether it be biological, material, or spiritual. The third chakra, the solar plexus, is the center of our individual identity, emotions, will, and our relationship with power. Ideas like "I" and "me," often called "ego," reside here. From this center we say, "I want" and "I will," and recognize or deny this right in others. Here too is our vulnerability. On the Soul Quest, powerfulness and vulnerability grow together: this prevents the abuse of power.

The fourth chakra, the heart chakra, is the loving center. Through it we give and receive love on the divine as well as on the human level. Every thought, every deed, and every action should be connected to and passed through this chakra. Anything that is said or done without love is better not said or done.

The fifth chakra, the throat chakra, contains our capacity to express ourselves and to communicate. People who have problems with communication often have blockages at this level. Visions, clairvoyance, and other transpersonal capacities are situated in the sixth chakra, the third eye. The connection with what is Highest is made through the seventh chakra, the crown chakra.

We can look at this system of chakras as a model of our potential for development. Each chakra can develop. As the chakras form a system of energy, their development needs to be kept in equilibrium. When one chakra is more or less developed than the others, the system is not in equilibrium and needs adjusting. We can use the chakra system as a means of diagnosing problems on the Soul Quest.

People who are out of equilibrium through having too little energy in the first chakra have difficulty grounding themselves and so they are unstable. They are dependent on other people for their stability and on others' energy-fields for their grounding. When we feel our energy being sucked out of us, it is often because we are in the company of someone with this problem. Because everything floats for these people, it is hard for them to achieve much. People with too much energy in this chakra have a heavy presence and little imagination.

When there is too much energy in the second chakra, people are controlled by their sexual urges. They are dominated by their need for instant and immediate gratification. This leads to a life and a sex life deprived of love, tenderness, and spirituality. Such a person needs to develop a better connection with the heart chakra. Too little energy in the second chakra means the person has difficulty being sexual, sensual, and creative. When this energy is suppressed this leads to problems, too. Many self-appointed gurus have problems in this area of their life: they become uncontrollable in their seductions of their young women and men disciples, proclaiming that they are bestowing favors! The only honest sexual relationships are those between people who are equal in every way.

People whose energy is concentrated mainly in the third chakra, the solar plexus, are likely to have their emotions and their need for power out of balance. Either they will be cut off from their emotions and will seek to gain power over and to dominate others, or their emotions will control them. These people need to ground their ability to feel emotions in the root chakra and to ground their need for power in the heart chakra. Too little energy in the solar plexus chakra means that the person's sense of identity is weak and precarious. Then the first task on the Soul Path is the establishment of a sense of identity. The use of techniques that challenge our sense of identity, such as meditation, Rebirthing, Regression and Reincarnation therapy, Voice Dialogue, and Bioenergetics, can be dangerous for people who are not clear about who they are.

People whose fourth chakra, the heart chakra, is too charged will quickly find themselves drained of their energy through giving too much, and will drain others of their energy through asking for too much. People with a weak or closed heart chakra cannot receive and give love.

If the fifth chakra, the throat chakra, is not in balance, our capacity to express ourselves and to communicate is impaired.

A person who is clairvoyant, intuitive, and insightful has a lot of energy in the sixth chakra, the third eye. When the other chakras are not equally developed, this person can be confused and deluded. Disequilibrium in the chakra system and a strong connection between the clairvoyant (sixth) and the power (third) chakras results in grandiosity, specialness, manipulation, the abuse of transpersonal abilities, and power-games. The functions of the sixth chakra need to be grounded in the common sense and simple energy of the root chakra, the creativity of the second chakra, the empowerment of the third chakra, and filtered through the heart chakra for wisdom's sake. The story of Cassandra shows a person whose clairvoyance was ill-expressed because she was energetically out of harmony and, in particular, disconnected from her second chakra.[4] Many people today who claim to be channels give strange and confused messages, and sometimes stupid and dangerous messages, because their sixth chakra is not grounded.

People whose seventh chakra has but little energy have no access to spiritual life nor to spiritual replenishment. Their energy is heavy and gray. Their lives and their behavior are not illuminated by higher thoughts, ethics, or the ideal of not harming others. Their lives lack grace.

The chakras and the aura or energy-field are the sense-organs of the subtle body. They are like radio stations that send out and receive messages. We communicate through them, both consciously and unconsciously. If we are not able to control the size of our aura and our chakras, their openness and receptivity, their force and permeability, we run the risk of being invaded and overwhelmed by other people's energy or of invading and overwhelming them. We are in danger of being submerged by too much incoming information. To learn to use the energy of the chakras and the energy-field is similar to learning a sport: it requires exercise, practice, and discipline.

Energy Cleansing

Every day our physical body is in contact with people and with the environment. At the end of the day it will have become more or less dirty, depending on the kind of work we do. It is certainly less fresh. Our energy-field, like our physical body, has been in contact with people and the environment throughout the day—in contact with their energy-fields. It too is affected. A part of the subtle energy that we have been in contact with remains in our energy-field in the same way that a part of the material energy like dust, for example, remains on our clothes, shoes, hair, and face. If we do not know that our energy body exists, are unaware of it and cannot feel it, we cannot keep it clean. Nevertheless, just as we protect our physical body with regular hygiene, nourishing food, baths and showers, clothes and shoes, we need to protect our energy body. Dirt left on the physical body long enough will lead to disease of the physical body, and dirt left in the energy body will lead to depletion of energy, disorder of the energy body, and disease of the physical body. Energy hygiene is Soul Hygiene.

All grounding exercises are exercises in energy hygiene and will clean the energy-field. Here are further exercises for cleaning the energy-field.

White Light

- *Imagine that your body is surrounded by a white light as dense as cotton wool and twenty centimeters deep.*

We can begin our day with this exercise even before we get out of bed. This visualization creates a coating of light which protects our energy-field. Each time we feel irritated during the day or feel that our energy space has been invaded we can repeat this exercise. Clients who work in offices practice this exercise every time they use the restrooms.

The Cleansing Breath

- *Sit in a comfortable, upright position, feet firmly placed on the floor.*
- *Feel your body. Notice whether there is tension in your head, neck, back, arms, or legs. Take your breath to the place that feels tense. Imagine that you collect the tension from that place with your breath and let that tension go with the exhale. Let it go gently or blow it out vigorously, whatever seems appropriate.*

When we train ourselves to be in constant contact with our breath and to understand the information it provides us with, we recognize very quickly when our energy-field has been soiled in one way or another. We can quickly re-establish its clarity through this exercise.

Golden Rain

- *Imagine that golden drops of rain are falling upon you. You are in a golden shower of rain. Feel these drops pass through your aura above and around your head: feel them touch your physical hair and your head. Feel these drops pass through that part of your energy body that surrounds your shoulders, your back, and your chest: feel the drops touch your physical shoulders, back, and chest. Feel the golden drops pass through your energy-body at the level of your waist, your hips, your buttocks: feel them touch your physical waist, hips, and buttocks. Feel the drops pass through your energy-field around your legs until they reach your feet: feel them touch your physical legs and feet. Let the golden drops run away, taking with them everything that does not belong in your energy-field.*
  You are well-bathed. Your aura is clean.

This exercise sends shivers of delight up and down both my physical and my energy body.

We live on Soul-level through the practice of ethical behavior and through awareness of the energy we are creating. Being careful with regard to our thoughts, words, and actions, we keep our energy-field clear and clean.

Here is an exercise we can do at the end of the day to clear the energy of our subtle bodies.

Energy Cleansing of the Physical and Subtle Bodies

- *As you lie in bed, before you go to sleep, take time to feel your physical body. How does it feel? Are there any parts that you are particularly aware of? Are these parts still connected with any events of your day?*
- *Take time to feel your emotional body. Are there any feelings in it that disturb you? How are they connected to the events of the day? Be aware of what you need to learn, so that these emotions can be released.*
- *Take time to feel your mental body. Are there any thoughts running through your mind that are connected with the events of your day? Finish them off and let them go.*
- *Good night! Pleasant dreams.*

We can do a similar exercise through the chakra system.

Energy Cleansing of the Chakra System

- *In your bed, or before you go to bed in a quiet place where you will not be disturbed, take several easy breaths and relax.*
- *Take time to be aware of your first chakra, near your perineum. Is it gently responding to your breathing? Is it comfortable? If not, is it still connected to people you met or places you went to or feelings you had during the day? Integrate what is necessary and let go what does not belong to you.*
- *Take time to be aware of your second chakra, above the pubis bone. Is it comfortable? If not, ask yourself what the discomfort means. Is it connected to other people in any way or does it contain other people's energy? Does it contain creative or sexual energy that you could not use during the day? Let go what does not belong there.*
- *Take time to be aware of your third chakra, just above the navel. How does it feel? Strong and radiant or blocked? Is it still connected to wishes and desires that you had during the day? Make clear decisions about how you wish to deal with them. When you have made the right decisions, this area will feel released and open.*

- *Take time to be aware of your fourth chakra, in the center of your body at the level of your heart. How does it feel? Safe and open or wounded and closed? Is it still connected to other people or other places? Go through your day and become aware of what your heart felt during the day. Forgive everyone and yourself. Tomorrow is the beginning of the rest of your life.*
- *Take time to be aware of your fifth chakra, near the top of your throat. How does it feel? Is it at all blocked? Go through your day and find what thoughts and feelings you did not express. Is it still connected with other people's energy? What aspects of their thoughts and feelings have become stuck in your throat? Let it all go.*
- *Take time to be aware of your third-eye chakra. Is it open enough or is it too open? Is it comfortable or uncomfortable? Do you feel informed about the "energy world," the world of intuitions and subtle sensations, or invaded by it? Have you paid attention to its messages during the day? If not, go through your day and pay attention now.*
- *Take time to be aware of your crown chakra. Connect all of your chakras with your breath. Breathe in to your crown chakra and release your breath through your root chakra. Let the crown chakra connect to whatever is your idea of the Highest. Surrender yourself and trust your night's rest to that.*

There are many other exercises for cleaning and purifying subtle energies which are well worth learning. They can be found in books by Linda Keen, Brugh Joy, and Barbara Ann Brennan, and in other books available today.

FOURTEEN

Skillful Empowerment:
Skillful Vulnerability

We Soul-Quest to feel inspired and to be inspiring, to achieve our potential and contribute to the world. We Soul-Quest to be empowered.

The great puzzle in empowerment is its relationship to Vulnerability. Many people think that being empowered means *never* feeling vulnerable. Surprisingly, on the Soul Path Empowerment and Vulnerability are equals. They grow together. That is why enlightened beings are compassionate. The more empowered we are, the more we recognize that we are vulnerable, without fear.

This is what Hal and Sidra Stone, who invented Voice Dialogue (see Chapter 21), say about our vulnerable subpersonality:

Perhaps the most universally disowned self in our civilized world is the vulnerable child. Yet this child may be our most precious subpersonality, the one closest to our essence, the one that enables us to become truly intimate, to fully experience others, and to love. . . . What is this child like? The most striking quality is its ability to be deeply intimate with another person. . . . The vulnerable child is tuned in energetically it is aware of everything that is happening. Words will not fool it for a moment. . . . This subpersonality can often tell us who is to be trusted and who is not. It usually recognizes

the people who have disowned their vulnerable children and who
can, therefore, hurt others, either accidentally or deliberately.
                    —*from* Embracing our Selves *(pp. 151f)*

Owning our Vulnerable Child prevents us from abusing our empowerment.

People who have disowned the vulnerable part of their personality do not understand what vulnerability means, so they equate empowerment with fighting. Their idea is, "The more empowered I am, the better I fight." They do not realize that we "fight" for Soul Quest causes without the use of violence. For them, vulnerability is a form of weakness, like asking for help, and this they dare not do. They confuse empowerment with being overpowering and they say, "I am responsible for myself, and other people are responsible for themselves. So if they cannot stand up for themselves and take their place, and I take it away from them, that's their problem. I'm not making any concessions." This is an abuse of the idea of self-responsibility. It is bullying and Ego Quest thinking.

People who disown their vulnerability cannot learn. They cannot ask questions, or say, "I do not know," or "I was wrong." These sad people can neither say, "It hurts," nor feel their pain nor ask for help. It is self-responsible to ask for help when we need it: there is no rule that says we have to suffer alone. People who dare not allow themselves to feel vulnerable cannot be truly intimate. Intimacy means closeness to ourselves as well as to others. It means awareness of what we and they feel and need.

Owning our Vulnerable Child permits us to grieve. Betsy was doing well on her Soul Path: she was crying all the time. Betsy's father had died when she was very young. She was the oldest child and her mother had told her, "Now you can be the man of the family." Betsy was the child upon whom all the responsibility fell. This frightened her so much that she cut herself off from her feelings completely for many years. At last, supported in a new and safe relationship and through good therapy, Betsy was empowered enough to feel and to grieve.

Having to deny that we feel vulnerable is stressful. Our human body is a vulnerable thing, vulnerable to illness, vulnerable to injury, vulnerable to old age and death. Our physical means for treading the Soul Path is fragile in its very nature. Ego may deny this, Soul does not. When we are truly empowered, we have no fear of our physical frailty and vulnerability. Grounded and centered, we can say, "It hurts me," without losing face or becoming disempowered. We have a great respect and carefulness for others. Our capacity to feel vulnerable is not weakness but strength and sensitivity.

Empowerment means being powerful and vulnerable in equal measure. Too much of one and we are dictators; too much of the other, and we are victims. Unless powerfulness and vulnerability are in balance, consciously or unconsciously we are playing power-games.

Ego thinks in comparisons: more or less, bigger or smaller, better or worse, you or me. It plays power-games. It sees others as dangerous and threatening so it seeks power in order to control and exploit them, and to prevent them from controlling and exploiting it. Ego believes that the more power it has, the less others have, and that that is the way to ensure its own safety. Ego is insecure; Soul is secure. Soul simply *is* powerful, and empowering. There is no competition on Soul-level, only cooperation. Soul does not know comparison: it just *is*.

As people become empowered, it is unfortunately not inevitable that they use their power well. Some use it to advance on their Soul Path; others, sadly, use it to devote themselves ever more strongly to an Ego-path. But Ego's power-games are self-defeating. People who live on Ego-level are frightened. Soul cannot be deceived, and everyone has some contact with Soul. Consciously or unconsciously, we all know the Boomerang Law. Power-game players know at some level that they are betraying their relationship with Soul. Consciously or unconsciously, they wait in fear for the return of the boomerang.

I always emphasize Ethics, the paving stones of the Soul Path. Becoming empowered is a responsibility that tests our ethics. In a fight, there are winners and losers—we are either one or the other. It is never ethical to disempower others. In empowerment there are no losers. Walking the Soul Path does not mean, "The more power I have, the less others have," but, "The more I am empowered, the more I empower others."

FIFTEEN
Skillful Consciousness

In Soul-Questing we are aware of many different states of consciousness: ordinary ones, spontaneous peak experiences that just happen to us, and particular altered states that require training to attain.

Our state of consciousness is the level on which we experience reality. Complicated theories exist, and sophisticated systems of states of consciousness have been described by Tart, Wilber, Grof, and others, but my favorite is the ONION. There is nothing theoretical about an onion! We cook with it. Preparing and cooking food is alchemy, and alchemy is synonymous with Soul Questing.

An onion has a skin, middle layers, increasingly fine inner layers, and a mysterious center that disappears the closer we get to it. How we experience reality depends on where we are on or in our onion.

There are Soul Quest tasks at each level of our onion.

When we are concerned with the usual ego boundaries and the limitations of time and space, we are occupied with *physical reality*. We measure and count, and believe that physically verifiable fact is "the truth." A good solid connection with this level of experience is a good solid contact with physical reality. Without it, our physical body is in danger: we need to be on this level to cross a road! Our mind, too, is in danger unless we are well-connected to this level: we cannot integrate the profound experiences that Soul-Questing brings when we are out of contact with physical reality. We become flippy or psychotic. The level of physical reality is also the level of common sense, keeping one's feet on the ground (grounding), discernment, and the right amount of doubt. It is the level where the influence of parents, society, genes, etc., is real. Blaming, too, is real on this level.

When we live in the reality created by our thoughts, we are in the *suggestion* layers of the onion, conditioned and programmed. We believe what we have been taught to believe, so what we can discover is limited. We experience reality as it has been suggested to us through socialization and education. Our thoughts truly create our reality on this level: we see what we expect to see; we do not see what we have not yet imagined. Placebo effects and unexpected recovery from serious illness happen here. As we transit from this to deeper levels, we go beyond our conditioning.

Deep in our onion are the *transpersonal and transcendental* layers where consciousness extends beyond Ego-level, time, and space. We observe our self in the process of being human. Our character is a process and we witness its unfolding through thoughts, sensations, and emotions: fear and confidence, love and hate, joy and sorrow, empowerment and weakness, shame and guilt, dependence and freedom, solitude and companionship, abandonment and unity, rejection and acceptance, the body as a biological entity and the body as pure energy, birth, life and death, shadow and light. We live these aspects objectively, in their purity, without seeking the comfort of connecting them to specific events. Accepting the kaleidoscope of our feelings without acting them out, we say, "When I feel abandoned, the feeling of abandonment is there. When I feel Oneness, the feeling of Oneness is there. When I feel hatred, the feeling of hatred is there. When I feel love, the feeling of love is there." We are conscious of our destiny or karma, the task of our Soul in this one among its many incarnations.

These are the least definable states of consciousness. They are sometimes described as direct contact with Soul, or God, or Oneness, or Universality. Sometimes they are called Emptiness, Nirvana, Buddha Nature. They come through disciplined practice. They come also by surprise. Our Soul Quest task is to bring their wisdom and holiness into our everyday life.

No one layer of our onion is "better" than any other. We need good access to our whole potential of states of consciousness. No layer is independent of any other. Each level gains in meaning through its relationships with the others. Each level of consciousness has its own functions, advantages, and disadvantages. Access to transpersonal levels enriches and deepens the way we live our human life, but without a good contact with physical reality, we cannot enter them safely or integrate our experiences there into our everyday life. To be limited to the outer layers limits choice and freedom and makes existence painful and incomprehensible. In Soul-Quest Alchemy, we need the whole onion.

This is a "cookbook" model of levels of consciousness, a simple, easy-to-use recipe. As we become Master-chef or Alchemist, we enter the different levels at will.

PART THREE

Soul Therapy Skills

On the Soul Quest, we are all teachers, we are all therapists, we are all students, we are all clients.

We all have something to teach: it may be as simple as sharing our knowledge or giving useful information; it may be a special insight or observation; it may be sharing an important experience.

We all have something healing to offer: it may be as very simple as common sense or practical advice; it may be a period of quiet and receptive listening.

We are all always learning, wherever we are on our Soul Path.

SIXTEEN
Skillful Teachers

When the student is ready the Teacher will come. As we develop Soul Quest skills, Teachers appear on our paths. Some are trained therapists, counselors, or group leaders. Some may have been trained in a religion. All teachers work within the framework of their beliefs and philosophy. To go to someone for therapy is to become their student. Therapists teach us how to work with and within their methods. We go to teachers and therapists who are good or corrupt, depending on what we have to learn and where we are on our Soul Path. Some students find corruption in the best of teachers; some clients do wonderful work with the most corrupt of therapists.

Teachers should be sufficiently advanced in their own Soul Quest to be able to guide another person in this task. They should recognize that each Soul Path is unique, and respect its individual rhythm, needs, and direction.

Teachers and therapists teach us Soul Quest skills to the extent of their ability.

> *A therapist is . . . what he has made of his experiences. What counts is not what has happened to him but what he has created from what has happened to him.* —Robert F. Hobson, *Forms of Feeling.*

A therapist whose self-esteem is low cannot help you to build self-esteem. A therapist who cannot maintain good relationships cannot teach you how to do it. A therapist who is blaming parents or society cannot support your self-responsibility. A teacher or therapist who is into power-games cannot support your empowerment. Whether you are choosing a therapist or a training, make sure that the person or people involved can teach what you want to learn.

The personality, qualities, and degree of development of teachers and therapists have at least as much importance as the techniques and the methods that they use. A method cannot give results beyond the ability of the person who practices it. Therapists are "wounded healers." Their basic qualification is their success in transforming the suffering and hurts of their own lives into something creative for themselves and others. We cannot help others where we have been unable to help ourselves.

Just as some people tend to look for father and mother figures—people who will take responsibility for them—they tend to seek gurus. Some teachers and therapists encourage their clients and students to treat them like gurus. This is disempowering. Some teachers and therapists take up a quasi-religious attitude towards the methods they use. This too is disempowering: it curbs a constructively critical spirit and limits progress.

On our Soul Path it is the journey that is important and not the destination. The most evolved teachers and therapists continue to be learners, to work on their process and to deepen their development. They may have achieved a certain level of development and learned a great deal. Nevertheless, they are always either at the beginning of the next step in their development or in the middle of it. Even though they have a repertoire of useful methods and techniques, they will have to learn new skills on this step. Teachers and therapists are always doing the same work as their clients: this is what enables them to help and understand.

Skillful Training

Teachers and therapists become qualified through working with other teachers and therapists in individual sessions, groups, and trainings. Experience in each of these is essential. There are important differences among them with regard to the level of attention offered, the commitment of the therapist or group leader, and our own commitment.

For everyone, individual attention is indispensable for development. Many people feel they have never received enough attention from parents, partners, at school or at work. In an individual session we receive full and undivided attention. As individual sessions are usually taken at the rate of one per week over a fairly long period of time, we also receive extensive support. This enables us to be profound about our development.

It is a logical step to work in a group after we have had a certain number of private sessions. Problems related to our personality and to our process of development present themselves differently in individual sessions than in a group. In a group we share the leader or leaders—the "parent" or "parents." Group work brings up problems related to family life such as sharing attention and love, and problems related to social life such as relating in a group, being companionable or withdrawn, and protecting our boundaries. We have to deal with the issue of trust and control. Our Soul Quest takes place here on Earth, among a group of co-inhabitants. If we wish truly to develop, it is indispensable to have a group experience. The more often a group meets, the more profoundly leaders and participants get to know and support each other, and the deeper their mutual commitment. The more supported we feel, the deeper our work.

A training takes more commitment than a workshop, and a long training takes more commitment than a shorter one. Lengthy trainings are traditional in Soul-Questing.

The goal of a training is that students become autonomous. They should achieve independence of their teachers, and competence in the methods they have learned and a constructively critical attitude towards them. They should have learned to regard their teachers with discernment, appreciating their qualities, recognizing their limits, loving them also for their faults, recognizing their essential humanity, seeing them as ordinary people. In this way both the students and their teachers keep their independence.

This is a maxim that I print out and give to students:

A good leader
does not create followers
S/he creates
more good leaders.

It is usually only in trainings that supervision takes place. The ideal of supervision in a training program is that it provides the trainee practitioner with support and guidance from professionals in his field while he is learning his skills. Professional therapists may go to other professionals for supervision. In the ideal case they do this with the sincere goal of advancing their self-understanding and enhancing their skills. Sometimes professional therapists go to each other for supervision in order to conform to the requirements of their professional body.

Supervision is essential in a training *and it has to be meaningful,* not just there for the rules, or done for self- or colleague-approval. Just as a good training will not necessarily produce a good therapist, the fact that someone is in supervision does not necessarily mean that they are advancing in their practice and development as a therapist or teacher. Instead of being empowering, supervision can be a battlefield for power-games. The quality of supervision depends on the development of the supervisors and on their ability to establish a relationship of trust with the students. Students who feel judged and threatened, rather than encouraged and supported, withhold information in order to protect their vulnerability and self-esteem. Honest supervision cannot take place under these circumstances.

There is no guarantee that someone who is "in supervision" is really receiving supervision. "Supervision" can be a sham. Many trainings treat supervision as a separate element—a certain number of hours which have to be filled to conform to recognition requirements. In these circumstances, much too often, there is no real supervision, just another workshop of whatever kind, called "supervision" to fill the requirement. Another way real supervision is avoided is when professional therapists go to like-minded colleagues they are comfortable with, rather than to colleagues who will challenge them. It is a myth, or at least an unsupported theory, that supervision improves the practice of therapists. Supervision can also be used to ensure that trainee therapists conform to the dogmas of their schools. Clive came to see what Rebirthing was about. He was in training to become an analyst and at the "separation" phase in his own analysis. I was very impressed by the way Clive could really let go into his breathing and by his capacity for awareness. In the first part of his session, he had the experience of Oneness. Then he had a past-life experience. At the end, when he was integrating his session, he said that he would not come back because, "My supervisor would not approve of these experiences." Clive was having brain-washing, not supervision.

In a training, real supervision cannot be separated from the process of development of the future therapist. It happens continuously and in relationship to every aspect of the work, to the extent that there is sufficient individual attention.

The purpose of supervision is that students should develop the integrity and empowerment necessary to be able to supervise themselves. They should develop sufficient confidence and perspicacity to recognize both where they do well and their limits, and feel safe to have limits—all therapists have limits. Recognizing one's limits means knowing when to consult others for help and advice, and when to go for further training and to acquire more skills. These days it is expected, and sometimes imposed, that serious therapists continue with supervision in various forms after their trainings and throughout their lives. This becomes a farce when therapists become addicted to supervision, or tell people that they are in supervision as if it proves that they are good therapists.

Supervision is linked with every moment of our life if we live consciously. The way we live as well as the way we work cannot be separated from our process of development. At its best, supervision is a form of awareness. We are continually aware of our dedication to the Soul Path, and self-supervise ourselves so that we remain upon it.

Skillful Teacher-Questor Relationship

There are basic rules that govern the relationship between Teacher and Questor, therapist and client. These are the same rules for Teachers as for therapists, for Questors as for clients, so I will use the words interchangeably in what follows. Both sides should know these rules. It is the responsibility of Teachers and therapists to ensure that they are maintained. Often it is part of the process of therapy that their Questors and clients test them. These rules concern sex, money, friendship, and therapy. The rules that concern sex and money are clear and ethically obvious, and I do not believe in exceptions. The rules that apply to friendship and therapy change according to where we are on our Soul Path.

Sexual relationships

Any form of sexual relationship between teachers or therapists and their students and clients is FORBIDDEN! It is an abuse no matter what the profession of the practitioner: doctor, psychiatrist, analyst, teacher, therapist, masseur, osteopath, naturopath, rabbi, or priest. *Anyone with any doubts on this subject is an addict to the Ego-quest and is not competent to accompany a path of personal and spiritual development.*

In therapy, clients let down their healthy, normal defenses. They are like children: trusting, innocent, and vulnerable. As in every relationship between adult and child, the balance of power and authority is in the favor of the adult. To relate sexually to someone in this unprotected state of consciousness is the equivalent of sexually abusing a child. Just as a child cannot take responsibility for entering a sexual relationship, so students and clients cannot, no matter what their age or experience of life. To permit such a relationship to seductive clients is to abuse their confidence. There is almost always a period in a process where the client or student sees the therapist or teacher as a parent. The child has the right to try to seduce its parent and, most especially, *the right not to succeed.* Children have the right *not* to be seduced by their parents.

An honest sexual relationship takes place between people who are equal. As long as clients and students still need their therapists or teachers, they have not become independent and autonomous. There is no equality in the relationship: the teacher or therapist has the power. Abuse of power is alien to the Soul Quest.

Many group leaders abuse their power by seducing group members. It is almost traditional! Some boast about it as a perk of the job. With such leaders, the group can only be dedicated to Ego-level.

Financial relationships

The financial relationship between the therapists and clients should be clear. The student or client is not the equal of the teacher or therapist in power and autonomy. Everything that is not clear in this relationship will exploit the client. Teachers and therapists should specify their fees and advise the client a sufficient time ahead of any changes. They should manage their finances independently of their clients, even when these clients are stockbrokers and bankers. They may never borrow money from a client or permit the client to pay for things for them.

Friendship and therapy

What about friendship? Everyone is our companion on the Soul Quest. Nevertheless, the relationship between therapist and client is a special one. On this subject there are ideals, but no answers. In classical psychoanalysis, this relationship is not allowed, and this causes many problems. In many of the new therapies the attitude is different and there is often an ideal about clients becoming friends. When I began to practice Conscious Breathing Techniques, I shared this ideal. (I would still like everyone in the world to be my friend.) In any case, my friends were my first clients. Then strangers came to work with me. I learned, through Jungian analysis, about the archetype of the therapist and the therapist-client relationship. My analyst promised me, "I will always be your therapist." At first I was suspicious. It felt a lot like a power-game and I always like to be independent. Then I realized that it was a promise that she would fulfill her task: she would be responsible for my therapy, and would not ask me to be responsible for hers. That felt wonderful. I was really free to come and use that time for me. Eventually I came to learn that this was an ideal and that she had her needs, too. At that point on my Soul Path it was good to learn this. I did not then have to ask of myself to fulfill an ideal of perfection.

Therapists can involve clients in their own therapy for many reasons and in different ways. They can be direct or indirect about it. When therapists have insufficient self-knowledge, they will use clients to act out and resolve their (the therapists') problems. There are examples of this in the chapters on Voice Dialogue and Past-Life Therapy.

The idea of the archetype of the therapist and its implications was very interesting to me. At first I thought that maintaining this relationship was all very well and wonderful for Jungian analysts and their clients, but what about people like me who have chosen to practice the new techniques, and who are humanistically and transpersonally oriented? We are more informal than most analysts, and we often do not call ourselves "analysts" or "therapists" even though we are doing the same work. Weren't we more ordinary, more accessible, less conventional and rule-bound? Could roles change, and in these circumstances, could a client become the therapist's therapist? Or did the rules apply to us too? In some schools of Rebirthing it is recommended that after a certain number of sessions, roles are reversed and the therapist gets a session from the client. The idea is that clients find this empowering.

Friendship is an archetype, too. There is a saying attributed to the Buddha which goes, "A good friend is the whole of holy life." While friendliness is an objective energy state—people either are generally friendly or not—true friendship only happens between people on the same level in their Soul Quest.

On the Soul Quest, we are all equals, all companions along the way. Some people know this already, others have to learn it. Among these equals, some are our natural friends, and others are companions with whom we have less in common. This is also true for the relationship between clients and therapists. Sometimes friendship is natural, and it just happens; sometimes it does not happen, however good the therapeutic relationship.

Real friends are mutual in caring. Clients do not come in order to care for their therapists, although many clients are naturally caring people. In therapy, the caring relationship should be one-way—not that clients should be discouraged from caring about their therapists, but that the caring remains part of the client's process, to be explored like any other part of their behavior. Caring is a relationship pattern and can be part of co-dependency. It is important that natural carers gain objectivity about this. They, in particular, must be discouraged from becoming their therapist's therapist.

When clients become friends, they take back their projections of the therapist's specialness and give up a one-way caring relationship. The therapist gives up the role of being special. The therapist gains a friend and the client loses a therapist. If this happens when the client is ready for it, nothing is lost and an ideal is achieved. A fully empowered person has emerged.

Being a friend means being equal. I teach in many countries, and I have noticed with interest that in hierarchical, more conservative, and conventional countries, I as therapist and trainer am "special"—whether I like it or not. As it so happens, I don't like it. In more egalitarian countries, I'm just another person. That is also how I see myself, so that is my preference. Clients in these countries are more independent and empowered.

SEVENTEEN
Skillful Questors

The client is the limiting factor for even the most gifted and highly qualified therapist. Unless the client is committed to the Soul Path, even the most Soul Quest-oriented teacher or therapist is helpless.

There are various reasons why therapy remains on Ego-level and never reaches Soul-level. Some purported teachers and therapists do not know that the Soul Path exists. Some clients do not want to make progress. They have a history of changing their therapist when the going gets too hot, which is when they risk becoming self-responsible. These clients know they are unhappy, and that they contribute to the unhappiness of the people around them, but they feel safer with the known situation than with the danger of the unknown that change will bring.

Kevin is about forty, a "soulful" type. (*He,* by Robert Johnson, is interesting on, and quite unromantic about, moods in men.) Kevin has read all the books about personal and spiritual development and knows the vocabulary well. Nevertheless, he is abusive to his wife and children, aggressive and blaming to his parents, and arrogant to colleagues. Every so often his wife threatens to leave and he fears his world will collapse. Then he becomes remorseful and goes into therapy. Kevin has no illusions about his behavior. He knows it is morally, ethically, and spiritually wrong. Through therapy things begin to change—and then

Kevin stops. Kevin is too selfish to give up his manipulations. He does not love others enough to care genuinely about their suffering. Intellectually he knows what the Soul Quest is. He reads books about it. But there is no commitment or integrity in his spirituality. It is abstract, intellectual, and meaningless.

It is not always wrong to change our therapist or to leave a training. We also change therapist as we develop.

If you have changed your therapist once or regularly, or have left a training, or if you do not feel you are making any progress on your Soul Path at this moment, here is an exercise in discernment which will help you to discover whether you have a vested interest in preserving the status quo in your life or whether you are willing to continue your development.

Am I Willing To Do Things Differently?

Part 1

- *Write down a list of what you know are your worst faults and failings. Try to own up to five of them. Be courageous. In what follows the "——" stands for the faults or failings on your list.*
- *Now write at the top of a page:*
  "Something that I would lose if I stopped being —— / doing —— / thinking —— / etc., is . . ."
  and then complete the phrase.

Example

- *"Something that I would lose if I stopped being manipulative / if I stopped blaming my mother / if I stopped thinking I was a failure / is . . ."*
- *Write as fast as you can all the ideas that come into your head without judging yourself. Then take the next item on your list.*
- *Now you know yourself better. You also have some idea of what your vested interests in staying as you are might be.*

Part 2

Now do the Good Energy Maintenance part of the exercise.
- *Write down a list of your good points and successes. List at least twenty.*
- *Now write at the top of a page:*
  "Something that I gain by being —- / doing — / thinking — / etc., is . . . "
and then complete the phrase.

Example

- *"Something I gain by being honest / by giving my mother as much unconditional love as I can / by thinking that I am successful / is . . . "*
- *When we value ourselves we are more easily able to develop than when we destroy ourselves with criticism.*

We are all clients or students. If we wish to develop and feel that we are not doing so sufficiently it may be that we need to change our therapist. It may also be that we need to be more willing to discover where, how, and why we are holding ourselves back.

Skillful Choosing

I once asked a group of my third-year students, all of whom had started as my clients, how they had made the choice to come to work and study with me. To my surprise—and somewhat to my horror—they told me that they were not at all interested my qualifications. "We came to *you*," they said. And there I was, running a four-year training in which they were participants!

What was I teaching my students? Theory and techniques, certainly, but most of all dedication to the Soul Quest.

I hope that this book will help you to choose. You may already have decided which qualities and competences you require in your teacher or therapist. Here are some further guidelines: be attentive to reputations, pay great attention to your instinct and intuition, and take into account the life-lessons that you need to learn—your Teacher or therapist should already have learned them.

Sometimes friends will tell us that their therapist is good, but we do not observe real and tangible results. Then we had better have the right amount of doubt. People put so much into their development—their time, money, courage, commitment, hopes, and ideals—that it can be difficult for them to admit to themselves or to others that they have wasted their effort. They may suspend their discernment and try to convince themselves as well as us that they are on the right path. If a friend is working with a teacher or therapist, or in a training, and you observe that your friend is becoming more successful in relationships, more content at work or finding a job that pleases better, more competent in money-management, happier in life, having more satisfying and joyful sex, you have evidence of good work. Good work leads to obvious results.

Your intuition is very important. It is your right to interview people you might choose to work with. Remember to choose your teacher or therapist with at least the same care that you choose your partner and your dentist. If you are not immediately enthusiastic about working with someone, don't do it. Even if the therapist is famous, gifted, inspired, and endowed with all sorts of qualities and has succeeded with all of your friends, it may be that at this time in your life, that person is not right for you. Follow your intuition.

Teachers and therapists who have not gone some way towards resolving a particular problem cannot help you to deal with it. Therapists who cannot manage their relationships, or money, or time, or education, cannot teach us how to be successful with ours. Therapists who cannot organize their life cannot help us to organize ours. It is reasonable to check up whether your potential therapist is competent in the areas where you require help. Make that part of the interview.

Remember that you have to have confidence in your therapist for the therapy to succeed.

EIGHTEEN
Skillful Working

Being a good teacher or therapist is a skill. Being an effective Questor, student, or client is a skill. Working at our Soul Quest is a skill. Skillful knowledge is necessary to live our lives on Soul-level. Knowledge brings empowerment and freedom. Good teachers, therapists, and methods educate; they do not indoctrinate. That is what sects and cults do.

Influence

Being influenced and influencing is part of life on Ego-level and on Soul-level. Our teachers and therapists influence us, as we inevitably influence those who regard us as teachers or therapists. Skillful working means awareness of how we are influenced. In almost all communication, there are elements of suggestion and manipulation, even in the communication of the most aware and responsible people who work hard to avoid it.

We all have conscious and unconscious strategies for controlling others. Many of the techniques that teachers and therapists use are intended to influence your way of thinking, by expanding your choices and helping you change unproductive habits. We can be influenced at Ego-level and at Soul-level. The former is disempowering, the latter is empowering. The following should help you to understand how you are being influenced so that you can be aware when it is happening and decide for yourself if you are empowered or not.

Suggestion

Techniques of suggestion are a powerful and creative therapeutic tool and are part of many methods including visualization, Eriksonian and other hypnosis, Neuro-Linguistic Programming, regression therapies, and past-life work. They are intended to be empowering, but it is easy enough to abuse them. Techniques can only be as honest and wise as the person using them. I once heard a therapist trained to advanced levels in Neuro-Linguistic Programming say, during a visualization he was guiding, ". . . and you will reach states of consciousness *with me* that you cannot reach on your own . . . ." This is an example of a disempowering suggestion: it creates dependency. When techniques of suggestion are abused, students and clients are being manipulated against their own interest. Be aware of what ideas are being suggested to you, and reject any that enhance the practitioner's authority to the detriment of your own.

Diagnosis is a form of suggestion. It can be positive or negative. If we are told we have an illness and will die within six months, it will take a lot of will-power on our part to survive any longer. If your therapist is telling you that you are not good enough, or don't function well enough, or that you have "severe problems," he or she is making disempowering suggestions. A therapist serves you better by recognizing your competence and teaching you how to learn from your problems.

Manipulation

Manipulation is an ugly word. It is what people do when they get us to do things that serve their interests rather than our own. There is as much manipulation in therapy as there is in life, and it is important to protect yourself from it.

In daily language, innumerable forms of manipulation are used consciously or unconsciously in communication. Something as ordinary and seemingly innocuous as a question can be a form of manipulation. When we ask someone a question, we guide their attention in the direction that we have chosen. It is easy to ignore accusations and labeling phrases which start, "You did . . . " and "You are . . . ." We have learned in childhood to shut out this unpleasant kind of communication all too frequently used by parents and in schools. But notice how difficult it is to avoid answering a direct question. When we are asked, "Did you . . . ?" or "Are you . . . ?" we cannot help but give our attention to the subject. Even in order to decide whether to answer or not, we are obliged to consider the question.

Therapists manipulate their clients. They have to: clients come to be manipulated beyond the limiting structures of their conditioning so that they can have new choices. They come to be outwitted: to be witted out of their unconstructive beliefs so that they can have more freedom and happiness. Sheila could not achieve anything to her satisfaction: she was a perfectionist. "There's no point in trying," she said, "as I won't do it well enough." "How well will you do it?" I asked. "Eighty percent," was her answer. Sheila and I had done several sessions together and I knew that I had her confidence. "Isn't that good enough for you?" I asked. "No," she was categorical. "Oh, dear," I said, "I don't know what to do now. I'm also a perfectionist, but eighty percent is acceptable to me, and I think my work is only that good. Do you still want to go on working with me now that you know this?" I manipulated her into the position where if she rejected herself, she would also have to reject me. She did not reject me, and became more satisfied with her own achievements.

"All is fair in love and war," they say. Soul Therapy is a war for freedom: freedom of choice, freedom to discern, independence, autonomy, freedom to be the person one really is. In ideal circumstances, therapists manipulate clients through beneficial suggestions truly for the client's own benefit and never for their own. When it is successful, teacher and Questor, therapist and client are winners; when it does not work, both are losers. Soul Therapy is the kind of a war in which either all parties win or all parties lose.

Interpretation

Interpretation is both suggestion and manipulation. It is a suggestion when it is made in the form of a proposition that clients are free to accept or reject. It is manipulation when it is made because therapists wants clients to see things their way—for the client's own good, of course!

Indoctrination

How can we trust that our trainings, teachers, and therapists are working with us in the direction of our healing and not manipulating us for their own convenience? It is always our responsibility to be informed. This book should help you. If you are learning about yourself and becoming autonomous and empowered, you have a good teacher or therapist. If not, have the courage to change.

This is the strategy of the most unconscionable manipulator I have ever observed in action. I'm pleased to say that he was not a therapist, but, sadly, he was a husband and father, and in a profession whose members should, theoretically, be highly trustworthy. Whenever someone said, "I would like to do . . ." and it did not suit him, he would reply in tones of surprise, amazement, and disbelief, "You don't really want to do that, do you?" Whenever someone said, "I think . . ." and he found this thought inconvenient, he would say incredulously, "You don't really think that, do you?" He used the same strategy when someone expressed needs that he found inconvenient. Because he was able to sound so genuinely surprised and disbelieving, he would destabilize the other person. He would skillfully manipulate them into self-doubt so that they lost entirely their confidence in their own knowledge of what they thought or wanted or needed. There is not much in this world that I consider downright evil: most of the time when people are hurtful towards each other I think it is through their own pain and ignorance. But this person knows what he is doing. Consciously controlling and manipulating others against their interests is truly evil.

If teachers or therapists are talking to you in this or in a similar manner, they are trying to brainwash you. If anyone with whom you are in a relationship is treating you in this way, they are trying to take over your mind. No matter where this is happening, get out of it as soon as you can. An institution or a person who treats you in this way is unscrupulous. Your autonomy and authenticity mean nothing to them. All they want is to control you and get their own way, no matter what price you may pay. Run for it!

Teaching

Trainings, teachers, and therapists teach us. The clearer they are about the teaching they are giving, the more obvious they will make its elements, offering these for our choice and consideration. This empowers us to choose the elements that are appropriate for us, and to reject others. Be clear that you are choosing to learn what you are learning.

Essential Concepts

Certain concepts in psychoanalysis have become part of almost every method of therapy. These are projection, transference, counter transference, resistance, and denial. Unfortunately these processes are often .abused in Ego-therapy rather than used creatively as part of Soul-therapy. It is skillful working to understand these concepts.

Projection

We "project" when we attribute to people or groups aspects of our own character that we reject or are not aware of. These may include positive or negative characteristics, beliefs, attitudes, judgments, and so forth. What we are projecting is our shadow: the part of ourselves that we are not conscious of and that we do not admit belongs to us.

How can we discover that hidden part of our personality? We may follow the way of pure detachment—if we are able—and sit for hours with our attention focused on our breathing in Zen or Vipassana meditation until we have gone beyond suffering and become Enlightened. But not many of us are capable of doing that. The way for most of us is rather through *projection:* through putting outside of ourselves what is inside. We need to cast our shadow so that we can look at it.

Meet Your Own Shadow

Part 1

- *Think of the two or three people that you like least of all, and make a list of the personality traits that you like the least in them.*

Part 2

- *Think of the two or three people that you like and admire the most and make a list of the personality traits in them that inspire you the most and which you would most like to have yourself.*

An exercise I often give in a group is to ask people to write a list of the qualities of the group members they like least. This is their secret list. They will never be asked to reveal it. Then I ask them to make a list of the qualities of the people they like most. When these lists are complete, each person reads their second list aloud, and discovers that they have described themselves. What they do with the first list is their own business!

There are both flattering and discomforting aspects of our personality that we are not conscious of and that we project onto others until we are self-responsible enough to take our projections back.

The process of projection works positively for us when we use it on Soul-level. It is our Soul Quest task to take back our projections.

Louisa complained that no one appreciated her, not her husband, or her parents, or her children, or her employer. "How do you feel about yourself?" I asked her, "Do you appreciate yourself?" "What should I appreciate myself for?" was her rather aggressive and irritable reply. Louisa discovered that she was attributing her lack of self-appreciation to her family. She could then work on her self-esteem, and do things for which she would be appreciated.

Our projections give us information about other people, too. We project because there is something in the other person that attracts our projections, a hook for us to hang our projections on. John was worried that his business partner was jealous of him. He worked on his own jealousy, which was directed against his brother and father. As John became clear about his jealousy, he was able to take a realistic view of that of his business partner and cope sensibly with it.

The function of projection on the Soul Quest is to make us conscious. It is then our discipline to be responsible for what we learn. People who refer to projection in a pejorative way have not understood its usefulness as a process of empowerment. Here is an exercise in taking back projections:

Taking Back Projections

- *Think back over your day today, and especially remember the people you met.*
- *What were your complimentary thoughts about them? What were your critical thoughts about them?*
- *Now see if you can find the same good points and faults in yourself as you found in others.*
- *Bravo for your courage!*

Transference

Transference happens when we behave towards our teachers and therapists as if they were some other important person in our life, such as our mother, father, sibling or other important family member, or school-teacher or other important person, and attribute to them the other person's thoughts, attitudes, and behavior. We are *transferring* attitudes and expectations from the situation in which they belong to another in which they do not belong. On an Ego Quest it is explained that we do this because we cannot help it. In Soul Questing we do this in order to become more aware. As with projections, we "transfer" in order to be able to look at what we are transferring and then to take it back—to stop doing it.

Paul told his therapist, "I feel helpless compared with you, just like with my mother." Julie was seductive to her therapist. She learned that that was her way of attracting her busy father's attention. Angela would not go to a woman therapist. Her mother had abandoned the family when she was five, and she associated all women with being abandoned. Paul, Julie, and Angela were transferring difficult childhood situations into their relationships with their therapists. They were repeating what had caused them suffering in order to become conscious of it, understand it, and integrate it.

Like projection, transference is a healthy, normal function. It is another form of casting a shadow that we can then look at. Here is an exercise to discover "transfers":

Taking Back "Transfers"

- *Think back over your day today, or your week. Was there an occasion when you got particularly upset? Remember in detail what happened. Write it down if this helps.*
- *Can you remember a parallel situation in your childhood or youth?*
- *Did your reaction today or this week belong to the event itself, or did it really belong to a childhood situation?*

Awareness will help you not to repeat "transfers."

Counter transference

Counter transference is the therapist's transference onto the client. It is the way in which the client affects the therapist. The client may remind the therapist of one of his own relatives, or a client's experience may remind the therapist of a similar experience of their own. Counter transference, too, can be an illuminating experience. It can teach the therapist how to guide the client on the Soul Path. It will only be positive, however, when the therapist is aware of his own process and can distinguish it clearly from that of the client. When therapists have insufficient insight, their counter transference can lead to abuse.

Relationships are a dance and counter transference is an element in the dance of relationships. It is the way clients get their therapists to dance with them, to respond to them. This way, they give their therapists clues. Jane observed that she was feeling maternal towards Cynthia, a client. She understood this feeling as a clue to Cynthia's need for mothering and found an occasion to talk to her about it. This led to constructive therapeutical work. David noticed that his client, Graham, reminded him of his Uncle Arnold. He remembered that nobody in the family took Uncle Arnold seriously. This clue made David realize that Graham's behavior made it difficult to take him seriously. He could then help Graham to recognize his unproductive behavior patterns.

When therapists have not done enough work on their own process, the counter transference obstructs the client's development. Claire, a student in a supervision session, complained that the client was trying to control her. "She just won't do anything I tell her to do!" she told me. Fortunately Claire has a sense of humor. When she heard her own words she understood.

Projection, transference, and counter transference are gifts when we know how to work with them. Therapists who are only capable of Ego Therapy use these concepts to control and manipulate their clients as part of their own power-games. Therapists with awareness of the Soul Quest understand how these processes serve it.

Resistance

The concept of "resistance" is all too often used pejoratively by therapists who do Ego Therapy. Clients are "holding out"—*resisting*—when they do not conform to the therapist's idea of how their development should go: they do not see what the therapist wants them to see, or say what the therapist wants them to say, or feel what the therapist wants them to feel, or remember the unpleasant events that the therapist thinks they ought to remember. Therapists use it to blame clients for not seeing things the therapist's way. The things the therapist sees may or may not exist. If they do, the important thing that is happening on the client's Soul Quest at that moment is that the client *does not* see, *does not* say, *does not* feel, and *does not* remember. Clients refuse for good reasons. Therapists use the word "resistance" when they have not understood their clients' messages and good reasons. It is a much-abused concept.

All of us are resistant some of the time. If we did not have ways to regulate the flow of unconscious material through our conscious minds, we would be inundated by both painful memories and glorious altered states of consciousness. We would be overwhelmed and unable to function in life. Resistance is useful. A therapist may discern that a client is unable to face the fact that a parent was abusive, or that a marriage is a failure—or that the client is herself a wonderful person. The client needs time and foundations before she can face these issues.

Clients are entitled to explore at their own rhythm. The work of therapists is to support clients, and not to control them. There are occasions where the therapist has observed well, and the client is unable to see something that the therapist sees honestly and clearly. What the undiscerning therapists would then call resistance is Soul protecting clients from becoming overwhelmed by material that they cannot yet integrate. The task of the therapist then is more acceptance, more respect, and more attention to building the foundations that permit the integration of suffering.

Denial

The concept of "denial" is the twin of "resistance." I once saw the phrase: "Denial is de name of a river in Egypt." Unfortunately this river is flooding over the field of therapy as the concept of "denial" becomes a term of abuse. Anytime a client disagrees with a therapist's interpretation, the client may be accused of denial. Anytime someone does not confess to being abused when a therapist thinks they have been, they run the risk of being accused of denial. Anytime anybody shows any doubt to a person who claims to have been abused, that person is likely to be accused of being in denial.

Abuse of Terminology

People who know just a little psychology prove the proverb that "A little knowledge is a dangerous thing." Having learned one or two concepts, they start to play *Psychological Insults*. They make remarks like "You're projecting," or "You're in denial." This is innocent enough, I suppose, in people who are learning about these processes for the first time. When teachers, therapists, or social workers have an inadequate understanding of these concepts and then play this game, they are dangerous. They are using these concepts to control their clients. In this power-game the therapist is the authority and the client is disempowered.

Another dangerous game is called *Psychological Diagnosis*. Here people who have read the odd book about psychological problems attribute diagnoses foolishly, as if they were terms of abuse. They say, "he's schizophrenic," or "she's psychotic" or "such and such a person is definitely borderline." When therapists use these terms in a derogatory or insulting way to distance themselves from their patients or clients, this too is dangerous.

A large part of the terminology of the psychoanalytic system of classifying people, used from Freud to Lowen, has come to have negative, pejorative, and devaluating connotations as much among analysts and psychiatrists who ought to know its limitations better as among lay people. Whenever we use this terminology, we run the risk of labeling suffering people as if they were objects and of depersonalizing them. We dispossess them of their humanity, individuality, vulnerability, and right to be themselves. All too often, labeling is used to justify cruel and immoral treatments.

Terminology and definitions such as "neurotic," "psychotic," 'schizophrenic," and "hysterical" have their appropriate place in the history of psychotherapy, but their validity has been surpassed by recent research and by new advances in the understanding of altered states of consciousness. Psychiatrists with a more compassionate and spiritual vision like R. D. Laing, Stanislav Grof, and Peter Breggin have found a Soul-Quest vocabulary for these experiences. Peter Breggin sees mental illness as a psychospiritual crisis. Stanislav and Christina Grof have created the beautiful and optimistic expression: *spiritual emergence*.[5] These new expressions offer a wider and more respectful vision of psychic suffering, and a wider vision always leads to more creative solutions.

I recently talked to an American colleague about the classification of mental illness. He said that Alan, a mutual acquaintance, was "sick" and should be medicated. In my terms Alan was in the middle of a spiritual emergency. I proposed rather gently to my colleague that there were in fact different views about mental illness. He immediately put me in my place: "There is a consensus opinion," he pontificated, "with which the vast majority of doctors agree and which obliges insurance companies to have to pay for treatment!" I could not help thinking that the people who create the consensus must also be those with a vested financial interest in the definition and existence of mental illness—as long as insurance companies are obliged to foot the bill. I am familiar with another consensus opinion: that of the very large number of teachers and therapists from many different backgrounds committed to doing better and to trying to understand with compassion rather than with labels—in other words, committed to the Soul Quest.

In these days of spiritual awakenings, we should be aware of the critical literature written against psychiatric definitions and categories, most of which is written by psychiatrists themselves. We should also be aware of Spiritual Emergence as a phenomenon of our time. Through being informed we may prevent unevolved practitioners from projecting onto us or onto people close to us their own mental problems and their lack of compassion.

Containment

In the beginning on our Soul Path our therapists and teachers "contain" or "hold" us. They protect us with their presence and provide the safe space in which we dare to feel our pain. In time, through becoming skillful at working on our Soul Quest, we learn to contain ourselves. We learn to be aware of what is happening in us, moment by moment, with enough detachment that we don't become identified with it. We become able to feel angry without getting carried away by our anger, sad without drowning in our sadness, vulnerable without losing self-esteem. Containment means being able to live well with ourselves even when we have to deal with unhappiness. There is no rule that says living on Soul-level means eternal happiness; it means full humanness, and that includes suffering.

No one has problems with happiness. When we are happy we forget our problems. We don't think of containment. We just live our lives. No client has ever gone to a therapist and complained of being too happy, or of being happy too much of the time. When people apply themselves to their Soul Quest it is always one of their objectives to become happier. Often, however, people are influenced by the "Wowie-zowie!" books and teachers who claim that if only we follow their method we will be happy, healthy, and rich all of the time—NON-STOP! This promotes the idea that we *must* be happy all the time, and that when we are not happy, something is wrong with us: we are *doing* something wrong. It must be our fault. How else is it possible that the promise of the key to successful relationships, self-esteem, creativity, empowerment, wealth, physical beauty, permanent youth, and beautiful altered states of consciousness (often all of this in only one weekend!) is not coming true? If any one method among the very many that claim to have solved all the problems of human suffering really had done this, we would all be following it. We are not stupid. Obviously, none of these claims stand up and none of these "Wowie-zowie!" methods work. Why not? Because they are not realistic.

Let's be realistic. Happiness and unhappiness are both part of human life. A person who has everything he or she could wish for—good health, a loving relationship with one's partner, good relationships with family members, rewarding and creative work and hobbies, and enough money—is happy. This happy person will see terrible human suffering on television every night and read about it in the papers every day and usually not be able to do anything about it. Is it possible to be completely happy in the face of that?

How do we cope with being unhappy? I ask clients at the beginning of a session how they are. They often say, "Fine," and force their face into a smile, as if this "Fine" is obligatory. Then I probe, and of course there is some pain, some unhappiness, some stimulus towards personal growth, otherwise the client would not have come. And somehow the client feels guilty about it. We have to learn to accept and be safe with our unhappiness. Accepting sadness and suffering means recognizing their role in our learning process. Of course we would like it to be otherwise: we prefer happiness to unhappiness. It always seems sad to me that we learn through suffering, and I console myself with the thought that without it there would be no compassion. We do not need to cultivate unhappiness: that is not a good thing to do. Skillful working means being able to accept our unhappiness in order to learn and to heal.

NINETEEN
Skillful Transformation

Experiences are transformed from Ego-level to Soul-level through integration and forgiveness. Integration means working with and taking the time to discover fully the meaningfulness of our pleasant and unpleasant experiences, how they happened, and their effect upon us. Forgiveness gives our experiences a different dimension.

Integration

Integration is normal. We are always integrating. In our process of development, our vision of ourselves and of the meaning of our lives changes, develops, and deepens. Even without any formal work or structured program of development our vision of our life will change with age and experience. The vision which we have of our parents, for example, at the age of six, is very different from the one we have when we are sixteen, which is, in its turn, very different from the one we have at twenty-six, etc. When we are six, for the most part, we accept our parents completely: they are everything that we know, our only examples. We need to think of them as being good. At sixteen we criticize and reject our parents and we fight against their values and the values of our society. This is necessary, because our personal growth work at that age—work which is difficult and painful—is to separate ourselves from our parents, to discover our own values, to find our identity and independence. At twenty-six we are often proving to our parents that we can do better than they can. At thirty-six we have discovered that, if in some aspects of life we are more successful than our parents, in others we are not. We notice that we even repeat some of their destructive behavior patterns whose faults we know only too well and for which we have severely criticized them.

Grieving, mourning, and feeling vulnerable are essential and inevitable parts of the process of integration. On our Soul Quest, as we accept our suffering and integrate it, we mourn for everything that we wished for but did not receive, and we grieve over everything that we received but which had no proper place in our lives. This period of mourning and grieving continues until we stop trying to escape from our suffering and face up to it. It continues until we have fully respected and accepted our suffering.

Integration takes time. Integration means recognizing the residue that painful experiences left in our mind and body, working through them, and healing their destructive effects. To integrate is to respect the rhythm of our process and not to do too much. Experiences that are not integrated are superficial mind-trips and intellectual pretensions—things we can talk about *ad infinitum* but which bear no fruit in our daily life. They are only words that we have learned to talk about ourselves. Each Soul Quest has its own rhythm. When we do not take time to integrate, the work we have put into our development results only in confusion, disillusionment, and problems.

There are many paths that lead to transformation. The one I have been most influenced by is the Four Noble Truths of the Buddhists.

The Buddhist Path to Transformation

The Buddhist path to transformation is called the Four Noble Truths:

1. *The Noble Truth of Suffering;*
2. *The Noble Truth of the Origin of Suffering;*
3. *The Noble Truth of the Cessation of Suffering; and*
4. *The Path to the Cessation of Suffering, the Noble Eightfold Path of:*
   Right View,
   Right Thought,
   Right Speech,
   Right Bodily Action,
   Right Livelihood,
   Right Effort,
   Right Mindfulness, and
   Right Concentration.

The Noble Truth of Suffering

Unless we can recognize and admit to our suffering, we have nothing to integrate. Our tendency is either to deny that we suffer or to drown in our suffering: blaming others and losing ourselves in self-pity and victim consciousness. When we are not really empowered, we have to prove to ourselves that we are good enough and so we cannot be humble. Then it can feel too painful to admit that our life is not going well enough, that our health is not perfect, that our relationships are not rewarding enough, that at work we do not have the success and the happiness that we hope for, that we have difficulties in communication, that our sex life is disappointing. When we admit that we are vulnerable and that we suffer, we stop running away from our unhappiness. We accept it and turn to face it. At that point we can integrate it. To integrate is to find a way of interpreting the painful events of our life which transforms our suffering into a lesson that we have learned, and which thereby empowers us and makes us happier and more creative.

We have many experiences every day and we think about them in order to understand them in the context of our life and of life in its entirety. We are always trying to understand ourselves and to explain ourselves, to ourselves and to others. The kind of questions we may ask ourselves during our day are:

- *Why doesn't my employer appreciate me, whatever I do?*
- *Why doesn't my wife/husband have any time for me?*
- *Why couldn't I have done better?*
- *Why am I ill at ease in this situation?*
- *Why couldn't I express myself?*
- *Why is this relationship also going wrong, like all the others have done?*

We nearly never ask ourselves questions like:

- *Why does my employer appreciate me so much?*
- *Why does my wife/husband love and appreciate me so deeply?*
- *Why do my children love and appreciate me?*
- *Why is this relationship going right, like so many others?*

We should, in fact, because we can learn a lot from our successes. Perhaps the reason is that when we are happy we don't ask ourselves questions. Suffering has some value: it makes us work on our Soul Quest. Some people begin their Soul Path in order to learn to live more effectively; some continue miserable until they cannot bear their suffering any longer, and only then commit themselves to Soul Quest tasks; some never begin Soul-Questing at all but continue to hurt themselves and others with their unsuccessful behavior patterns without being able to take a detached view. Is it because they have not suffered enough?

The Noble Truth of the Origin of Suffering

Our next task is to recognize where our suffering comes from. This means going back to the repressed incidents that have hurt us, accepting them, integrating them, and learning how they have served our Soul Quest. Once we discover and integrate the answers to our questions, these responses have a great effect on our life and on the vision we have of ourselves.

Here's an example: Norma thought that her employer did not appreciate her. As she worked on her development, she discovered that she had never felt appreciated by her father, and that this experience had led to her to the conviction that she held and often repeated to herself, "Men don't appreciate me." When she discovered this element in her conditioning, this conviction dissolved. She became aware that she had a different relationship with each of the different men she knew, and that some of these men appreciated her while others did not. Through being realistic, her relationship with men improved. Her work of integration consisted of reconstructing her way of relating to men. She needed to be aware of and attentive to her old behavior patterns and to observe and to discipline herself so as not to repeat them. She needed to choose and to discover her own constructive way of making a relationship with a man, rather than repeating the habit of relating to men that she had learned with her father. Time is always needed to integrate such a radical change.

The Noble Truth of the Cessation of Suffering

If we want our suffering to cease, we have to recognize fully how it has affected us. Our painful past experiences have conditioned our behavior in the present. They are part of the program of who we are now. Our suffering influences our thoughts and attitudes and influences our breath and bodily functions and the illnesses that we suffer from. Recognition leads to acceptance, integration, and finally, to freedom from the conditioning and from the suffering.

Vulnerability

Sometimes people are ashamed of feeling vulnerable, as if it proves that they are "bad" and "worthless." This makes it difficult for them integrate their suffering and to come free of its effects upon them.

I have placed a great emphasis on vulnerability here and in many places in this book. If we cannot feel vulnerable we are in flight. We flee into anger, grief, joking, blaming, reasoning, explaining, insulting, or in any number of different ways—anything to avoid admitting that "it hurts" or "I hurt." When we really are strong, it is not a problem to be with our pain without explanation and justification, in full self-respect and self-esteem, to say "It hurts" without feeling diminished. Without that it remains unintegrated. To flee our vulnerability is to flee our Soul Path.

Vulnerability Exercise

- *The next time you feel angry or sad, or want to joke, or to blame, or you hear yourself reasoning and explaining in a tense manner, or you want to hurt or insult someone else, take time to become aware of what is hurting you. If another person is involved, try to tell them, "I hurt."*

When we know that we hurt and can accept it with dignity, we are truly empowered.

Suffering

Sometimes people feel ashamed of their suffering. Then they may resort to explaining and justifying it or to excuse the people who have caused them suffering, identifying with their oppressors. This will lead them to say, "My mother rejected me *because she had been rejected by her mother.*" The reason why we may have been rejected by our mother does not matter to our wounded Inner Child, who remains wounded until its pain is integrated by the adult that we now are.

The adult part of us justifies the hurtful behavior of others through making excuses and providing the historical contexts. It attempts to dilute our suffering through explanations and justifications. When we limit our account to the simplest phrases, and say only, for example, "My mother rejected me. My mother could not love me. My mother had no time for me," we allow ourselves to feel our suffering in its fullest intensity with all the pain and emotion and vulnerability involved. Only in this way can we integrate our suffering.

Sometimes we seek to blame the people who have hurt us. We may say, "My father was a bully *and it is his fault that I cannot stand up for myself. It's his fault that I feel worthless."* Through blaming, too, we attempt to dilute our suffering; we push it away from us. It is much more empowered to say simply, "My father was a bully. My father told me I was worthless. I cannot stand up for myself." Then we truly attend to the pain and integrate it.

While it is right to see that our parents are ordinary people just as we are, and that, for the most part, when they have caused us suffering, it was their ignorance and their own suffering which made them unable to do better, *this does not change the fact that we suffered.* If someone stands on our foot by mistake, it still hurts. Excusing and blaming do not lead us to integrate our suffering: they reinforce our patterns of suffering.

Here is an advanced exercise for recognizing and thus respecting and integrating our suffering.

I Recognize My Suffering

- *Find a friend who can listen empathetically without intruding with her or his own story, or be such a friend to yourself and do this exercise on your own. Tell your friend or yourself,*
  "In my life I have suffered . . . ,"
  and begin your account.
- *The rules for this exercise are very strict. You are* not *allowed to do any naming and blaming of anyone who you identify as having caused you suffering, nor any offering of excuses and explanations for them or for what they did to you. That is* their *story and you are to tell yours.*
- *When you can do that you will have integrated your suffering.*

In this exercise we have to be very simple to succeed. Begin your account, "In my life I have suffered. . . ." Listen to your words. Recognize your suffering. Feel your vulnerability. Develop compassion for yourself.

Evelyn was the original good daughter. She thought that if only she had been able to comfort her mother sufficiently, her mother might not have been so miserable—here Evelyn is talking about a time when she was eight to twelve years old! Or if only she had been a boy, her father would have been more patient with her. Evelyn cried, and blamed herself for crying and became irritated with herself for crying—after all it was all her fault—and could not stop crying. I asked her, "Tell me about your suffering without any explanations or justifications. Just tell me, 'Joy, I have suffered. . . .'" Evelyn did that, and for the first time had a chance to hear herself and respect her suffering. It was a turning point on her Soul Path.

The Path to the Cessation of Suffering: Ethics and Forgiveness

The path to the Cessation of Suffering is, of course, our Soul Path with its paving stones of Ethics. We discipline ourselves to be careful of our behavior in thought, speech, and action. This way we avoid creating more suffering in the world.

Most people have good intentions about following an ethical path, and then find that they cannot fully do it. They make the resolution to be caring to their partners, patient with their children, efficient at work, careful of the environment—and find that nothing changes. Our behavior does not change through good intentions or through will-power. It changes when we are able to forgive. Until we have forgiven we will be drawn to revenge, and revenge has no place on a Soul Path. We hurt ourselves as well as others, so we need to forgive ourselves as well as others. Here are four affirmations that help with forgiveness. I learned these beautiful affirmations through Rebirthing.

> 1. *I forgive myself for having hurt others.*
> 2. *I forgive others for having hurt me.*
> 3. *I forgive myself for having let others hurt me.*
> 4. *I forgive others for having let me hurt them.*[6]

Forgiveness does not happen through merely repeating words or writing affirmations, although these practices are useful. We cannot forgive anyone until we know fully what we have to forgive them for. Forgiveness can only happen when we have integrated our suffering.

Transformation

This process of transformation works for physical, emotional, and spiritual suffering.

The Transformation of Physical Suffering

Laura's suffering came through her body. She had never been strong physically. From birth there was something wrong with her bones. She needed many operations to remedy the problem. In therapy she remembered the hospitalizations, the separations from her family and friends, the operations, the periods of recovery, the physiotherapy, the mental and physical pain of having large scars on her legs. Laura was in her early thirties. She came to me because somehow, for reasons she did not understand, she was losing courage. Laura took time to integrate the many effects of her ailment on her life. In time she became able to take a higher view of what had happened. Through her ailment she had been forced to be aware of and careful about her health. She would have liked to become a physiotherapist, but lacked the physical strength. Instead she had become a nutritionist, and had developed a very successful career. When she could appreciate how well she had always coped and recognized how useful she was to others, Laura became aware of the quality and the sense of her life. She saw how her physical suffering had helped her develop as a person, and had been instrumental in her success on her Soul Quest.

The Transformation of Emotional Suffering

Meryl's suffering was on the emotional level. She had suffered a lot in her relationship with her mother. She knew her mother never wanted her and, naturally, she felt rejected. Meryl remembered being mistreated by her mother and experienced many emotions: abandonment, sadness, panic. A child depends on its parents for its life, and a child that is not desired has a sense that its life is in danger. For a while Meryl was preoccupied with her resentment, anger, and hatred towards her mother. These strong emotions protected her from feeling vulnerable. Meryl recognized how her suffering was affecting her everyday life. At that moment she had to choose whether to go on blaming her mother or to forgive her. To blame meant to continue to see herself in the role of victim and her mother in that of oppressor. How could this serve her Soul Quest? Meryl learned to contain her sorrow, and came to integrate her suffering. The more she accepted her feelings, the more she respected the reality of her suffering, the more she dared to feel vulnerable, the more she became empowered. Then in a moment of grace, through a vision, Meryl perceived her mother's woundedness. Instead of feeling that she was her mother's victim, she felt compassion for her mother. Gradually she understood that the way her mother had treated her had made her aware of other people's suffering, considerate and sensitive, and that, through bringing her into therapy, it had furthered her Soul Quest. In that way she transformed her emotional suffering.

The Transformation of Spiritual Suffering

We are spiritual beings. When we are wounded physically and emotionally, we are also wounded on the spiritual level. When we are babies, we are in good contact with ourselves. We feel our feelings: when we are hungry, we demand to be fed; when we are suffering, we cry and expect to be attended to; when we are angry, we yell. We do not hold back. We are adorable, spontaneous, trusting, and completely self-centered. We are energy bombs, and we are too much for our parents, with the exception perhaps of the most developed and enlightened among them. Having been repressed by their parents, our parents repress us. They live demanding lives and are under pressure, and as we grow up, they cannot cope with our directness, the clarity of our vision, and the intensity of our love and hatred. Little by little, they disempower us. When we say about Auntie Ann, our mother's sister, "Mother, I don't think Auntie Ann likes you very much!" our mother denies it. She cannot admit this painful truth to herself. How then could she admit it to her child? She tells us we are wrong, and we lose confidence. Such incidents continue until we are cut off from our inner knowledge.

As young children, we are not conscious of our abilities. We have no introspection or conscious awareness. We live in the present. We do not evaluate ourselves and so we do not recognize our gifts. We do not know that we are intelligent, kind, thoughtful, perceptive, intuitive, visionary, vibrant with life. We cannot assert the existence of these capacities—we do not even know their names—and so we cannot protect them when they go unrecognized by others. We cannot answer our parents or our teachers, "No, mother, I am not selfish," "No, father, I am not irritating," "No, teacher, I am not distracting," because we do not even know what it means to be these things or not to be them. This is why it is possible for us to become cut off from our capacities and our abilities and to end up unconscious that we have them. Our task on our Soul Quest is, as always, to become conscious of our qualities, of the value of our intuitions and insights, of the depth of our knowledge, of the reality of our wisdom, of the truthfulness of our visions. Little by little, always at a deeper level, we regain for always these important parts of ourselves. We recognize them and we protect them. Grateful and conscious, we come to know who we really are.

This is the transformation of spiritual suffering.

PART *4* FOUR

Skillful Methods

Traditional Soul Quest methods include prayer and worship, observing commandments, performing rituals, sacrifice, meditation, yoga, and use of sacred substances that lead to altered states of consciousness. During the last twenty to thirty years, new methods that purport to be therapeutic and spiritual have proliferated. In such an abundance we feel confused and overwhelmed. Each new method is presented with more enthusiasm than the last and with more exaggerated claims. Proselytizers are not concerned with the limits of their method, but with attracting a following. No method is right for everybody. It is a Soul Quest task to find those that help us advance on our Soul Path.

Choosing among the new methods is difficult. While there is a lot of propaganda, there is usually little real information available. We have to do our own research and become informed consumers. It is reasonable to ask our prospective teachers or therapists how they came to choose the methods they use, what problems these methods have helped them to solve, and what problems they cannot help with. In psychiatry, for example, it is well known that drugs always have side effects: their use has to be weighed up against patients' ability to cope with their suffering without drugs. Methods from earlier times were not inevitably successful. Trainee shamans often died and novices often left monastic orders. New methods too have limitations. Some also cause side effects in their practitioners—mostly flippiness (lack of grounding), conceit and inflation (absence of humility).

I am not informed about all of the new methods. The techniques I describe here are those that I have benefitted from on my own Soul Quest and that I also practice and teach: Conscious Breathing Techniques including Rebirthing, Voice Dialogue, and Past-life Therapy. I tell how I discovered these methods, and what I think their strengths and limitations are. As I am doing my most innovative work through Conscious Breathing Techniques, they will receive the most space. This does not mean that the others, or other techniques and methods that I have not mentioned, are less valuable.

I hope my approach to the information I give is useful to you. It should give you an idea of questions to ask and of how to be discerning. Therapy is a battle for the Soul and methods should reach the Soul.

TWENTY
Conscious Breathing Techniques[7]

*In many different languages there is often a clear and close corre-
lation between the words for breath and breathing and the words for
soul or spirit.* —Minett, Breath and Spirit *(p. 144)*

*Meditation is a process of holding the attention upon a wholesome
object. The breath is such an object.* —Brazier, Zen Therapy *(p. 67)*

The first Conscious Breathing technique that I worked with was
the Buddhist Vipassana meditation in 1965. Many years later, in
1986, I was trained in Rebirthing and I developed this technique
in my own way, influenced by Buddhist breathing exercises and
by my experience of Jungian analysis. Through combining these, I
have created a gentle way to use Conscious Breathing techniques
in Soul-Questing and now formally call what I do "Conscious
Breathing Techniques."

I discovered Rebirthing in 1984 in London. At the time I was
going through a painful divorce and needed support. A friend
introduced me to a therapist who was a Rebirther. I liked and
trusted her and I decided to work with her. I knew nothing at all
about Rebirthing. In my first session I relived my birth. This was
such a disagreeable and violent experience that I said, "If this
happens every time, I'm not coming back!" In the second session

my chakras opened up one by one and the universe was making love with me. Before that experience, probably having more than the right amount of doubt, I had thought that chakras existed only in the imagination of people with fantasies about India.

Rebirthing opened up a whole new world of people committed to the Soul Quest and participating in it joyfully. The experiences were pure Soul-level. I work hard in all that I write about Breathwork to be moderate and balanced. Let me tell you about the Conscious Breathing session I gave just as I was putting the finishing touches to this chapter.

Gordon has cancer. He has been fighting it for several years now, and after a long remission, it came back. Gordon was angry and afraid, all the more as two of his friends had recently died of cancer. This was his first Conscious Breathing session. In the beginning I could see much anger in his breath. "Tell me," I said, proposing a variant of the Listing Technique, "One thing I am angry about is. . . . Just become aware of your anger." Gordon said slowly, through his teeth, "I'm not angry. . . . I am so angry . . . with myself." He relaxed and his breath became more coherent and smoother but he was still making the large inspirations and expirations that we make when we are pushing our feelings away. "Let your breath become smaller," I suggested, "Let it be softer. Let your body provide the rhythm." Through his extensive experience in meditation, Gordon could let go. Then his breath took over and breathed him. He saw colors—pink and violet and yellow—and energy began to flow through his body. For a while it shuddered and shook, always gently. Waves of energy went through his legs. Then his hips began to rock gently. His body gave itself what he later described as gentle osteopathy for his usual backache. Then his body went quiet. Gordon spontaneously put his hands over the area where the cancer was coming back and let his energy flow through them into it. This energy balancing went on of its own accord for an hour, and I had nothing more to do or to say. Eventually Gordon opened his eyes, radiant, glowing. He hugged me tightly, grateful for his experience. There was nothing to talk about, nothing to discuss;

integration just happened. It was so simple. "I'm going to walk in the forest," he said, and left.

Gordon's cancer did go into remission again after that session, but—wonderful as this is—it is not the central issue here. If it becomes the central issue, we fall into the trap of spiritual materialism. We do not Soul-Quest to heal a specific disease: we Soul-Quest to learn to live on Soul-level. When that heals our diseases, that is a bonus. Gordon is an advanced Soul-Questor. He knows how to use his cancer to advance on his Soul Path. What is important in terms of Breathwork is that what happened came about without effort, that it was what Gordon needed at that moment, and that afterwards he was happy, radiant, and glowing. So was I and so were two observers who had come to watch me work.

I will still try to be as moderate and balanced as I can be about Conscious Breathing Techniques. I don't want to join the people who make wild, unfounded claims in order to seduce others into following their methods. But I also don't want to err in the other direction and give a diminished and excessively moderate picture of what Breathwork can achieve. The proverb says: *Life is in the breath. He who half breathes, half lives.* What I have observed is that

THE PATH OF THE SOUL IS THE BREATH.

I use other methods, many of them. I am not a fanatic about Conscious Breathing Techniques and I certainly do not proclaim that this is the "only" way. But before I use other methods I teach people how to use their breath. Clients can go further with every other method when they know how to use their breath to support their process.

How I Was Taught Rebirthing

I was taught Rebirthing as a breathing technique in which the in-breath and the out-breath are connected, and the breath is strong and rapid high up in the chest—almost like panting. If you spend a moment observing your breathing you will notice that there is a pause between in-breath and out-breath, and again between out-breath and in-breath. This is normal in an adult. Rebirthing tradition, or mythology, says that an infant spontaneously does connected breathing (I have not verified this), as do people who are at ease with their breathing. I do not know of any research to test this claim. I know that when I feel good *and* remember to observe my breathing, I notice that it is connected, and I associate feeling good with connected breathing. But this may be pure coincidence. Like most people, when I feel good I get on with my creative life and do not stop to observe my processes.

In my first Rebirthing sessions in England and in my training in Spiritual Therapy in Holland with Hans Mensink and Tilke Platteel-Deur, this fast, connected breathing that happened high up in the chest was "Rebirthing." Tilke worked on the principle, "The more air there is, the more opening there is," which is an effective Breathwork technique. Hans is more "laissez-faire" and laid back. From both I learned to be confident in my breathing, to surrender to it and to let it lead me.

Throughout the first year of the training, Hans and Tilke let me follow the path of my breathing without interfering. In almost all of the sessions in that first year my breathing was as light as a butterfly, fluttering in my chest like a pulse, from time to time almost invisible. Once my breath fluttered in my third-eye chakra, which was very pleasant. During my sessions I was always in high, "spiritual," altered states of consciousness.

There are people who start Rebirthing by dealing with their emotional problems. Sessions are tearful. There are regressions to painful moments in infancy and childhood including the reliving of the birth trauma, the characteristic experience which gave Rebirthing its name. For others, facing their pain is too frightening and so they start with spiritual experiences and afterwards confront their personal suffering. If they fail to ground and integrate these spiritual experiences they remain flippy and disconnected, and unable to live in the real world. At the beginning in my individual sessions, my process included a mixture of emotional and spiritual experiences, but during almost all of my first year in the training I only had spiritual experiences. I needed these to build up enough confidence in the group to dare to have emotional experiences "in public." Only towards the end of the first year of the training did I dare to breathe in a more physical way. Then I discovered my vulnerability, my emotions, my feelings, and my body and began the painful process of grieving for my father who had died thirty-five years earlier when I was six. You can see that I know about the problem of incarnating from my own experience!

Thank you, Hans and Tilke, for your patience.

My Encounter with Tetany

The method of breathing in which the in-breath and the out-breath are connected and the breath is strong and rapid high up in the chest is sometimes called hyperventilation. Rebirthing is often associated with hyperventilation. Rapid upper chest breathing or hyperventilation can lead to an opening of consciousness on the emotional or spiritual level. It can also lead to tetany—rigid and painful hands or a tight, unmovable mouth area. Tetany may last for the whole session—three-quarters of an hour to one hour and a quarter—and can be repeated for session after session. I often saw tetanies in the training in Holland and in other groups, although these happened rather seldom with my clients except for the occasional macho who had to force his breath to prove something. I have never suffered from tetany. Once in a session the Rebirther pushed me too far and tetany began. I felt the pain in my hands and looked at them with fascination. They were quite stiff. "Oh, look," I thought, quite excited at last to have this notorious experience, "this can happen to me too!" I was amused. And then I thought, "This is ridiculous. I'm not going along with it. I am not a masochist." I stopped following my Rebirther's instructions, changed my rhythm of breathing, and the tetany went away.

There is emotional pain on the Soul Quest as we discover the ways in which we have been hurt and go through the process of grieving, mourning for our losses, recognizing our inadequacies, and becoming self-responsible. Through the strong techniques that bring on regressions we relive physical pain too. We may relive an operation, or a time when we were physically attacked or had an accident. We may be forced into reliving pain by therapists who use techniques aggressively, or who are addicted to pain. Pain can be a habit—our therapists' or our own. Unless pain arises spontaneously through a gentle technique, we had better ask ourselves why we are experiencing it: why we are acting out the scenario, "Life is painful."

Professional Practice

I became a professional Rebirther and practiced in the way modeled by Hans and Tilke. I taught the method as I had learned it, but when the breath was in a place other than in the chest, and had another form than connected, I accepted it. I never pushed my clients into forced rapid breathing rhythms. I also gave my clients time to talk and I listened. My first Rebirther had given me a lot of time to talk and I had learned the importance of being listened to. Now I know that this is the reason why so few of my clients went into tetany: intuitively I was giving them time to build up trust in me and to prepare a secure foundation for their Soul Path.

The effect of Rebirthing, in many cases, mine included, is an opening of the unconscious which happens very quickly, often in the first session, and brings about experiences which range from powerful regressions to traumatic experiences, to the attainment of ecstatic altered states of consciousness. By the end of 1988 the effect of my Rebirthing experiences was that I did not feel good. It felt like the part of me that I call "I" was going to get absorbed into something much bigger and become lost forever. I was far away from Hans and Tilke and my fellow students, in a new country, Switzerland, learning a new language, and commuting to Holland to continue the training. I met a Jungian analyst, and decided to enter analysis. Analysis helped me to develop a sufficiently grounded and incarnated ego that was no longer afraid of becoming lost in Soul.

The world of personal and spiritual development has been much influenced by Indian religion and philosophy. This influence has not always come through studying original texts or consulting experts. Unfortunately, most often, it comes from the projections and inventions of self-appointed gurus. A sort of pop spirituality has been produced that people who wish to show themselves "spiritual" repeat. They gabble fashionable jargon about "surrender," "going beyond Ego," or "trust" but have no idea what these expressions mean. The teachers who have really understood what going beyond Ego is know who they really are. They are not in an identity or existential crisis. People who do not know who they really are have nothing yet to go beyond! Many of the new techniques, and certainly all of those that use the breath, are capable of bringing us into altered states of consciousness that were only attainable after years of practice in the ancient traditions. What will we "do" with these altered states of consciousness? Will we integrate and become enriched by them or will we become flippy and conceited? I have seen people do both.

Rebirthing easily brings unconscious material into consciousness. For the result to be integrated, we need a strong Ego, a strong sense of who we are: there has to be an "I – me" who undertakes the Soul Quest. Change and development happen in relationship to this sense of self.

The hysteria frequent in Rebirthing groups had always been a problem to me. Many people would get disconnected for longer or shorter periods. This was taken for granted by the group leaders and other participants, but I wondered and worried about it. (I later learned that excessive emotionality and disconnectedness was a characteristic of many personal growth groups of the 1970s and 1980s!)

As a new and inexperienced Rebirther, I worried too that my private clients trusted me so much that often in their very first session they would have the strongly emotional regressions to early suffering that are so typical of Rebirthing. My practical side was asking, "What is this good for?" I could not "just believe" or "trust the process." My instincts were saying all the time, "Too fast! Too fast!" My results were good in terms of what I had been taught and in the context of the usual Rebirthing experiences, but I felt dissatisfied. I kept thinking that something better could be done.

Then came a turning point. Thomas opens up easily through Rebirthing. In our fourth session he found himself regressed to the age of four, when, away from home, he had been shut up in a small basement room and had escaped through a window. His regression was so strong that after he relived the escape he did not recognize me but wandered around the room, lost and terrified, calling pitifully, "Mama, Mama." Finally, he sat by the foot of the sofa, despairing, cut off from the world, autistic. I was horrified: it is never easy to see a person relive an experience of such suffering. I was also frightened: what if Thomas became lost in this unconsciousness? To my great relief, Thomas gradually came to recognize me and became again a reasonably competent adult. It took several sessions, however, before he integrated his autistic part, and that was not through Rebirthing, but because I use art therapy and other skills. Thomas refused to do more Rebirthing for a while. What would have happened to him if my only training was in Rebirthing? The effect on me of this session was profound and remains so to this day.

On the Soul Path, it is normal to be unsettled from time to time and to have one's behavior patterns destabilized. All change affects us more or less strongly, including ordinary events like moving house or changing job. A manageable quantity of destabilization—one that we can integrate—has a healing effect and leads to new and better ways of thinking and living and to new solutions to old problems. But to be completely destabilized as Thomas had been . . . I could not accept that that should happen again with another client. I did not want to do work that had that kind of outcome. There *had* to be another, better way of working. It had to be possible to attain good results gently. It must be possible to keep the effectiveness of Rebirthing but to manage it better so that it led to more grounded outcomes.

Experiments

I wondered what would happen if instead of asking clients to do strong, rapid, upper chest breathing, I asked them to do connected breathing in a spontaneous rhythm. I began to give the instruction, "Let your body breathe. Respect its rhythm, observe it, follow it, and then, when its natural rhythm is established, make your breathing connected."

I noticed that the body provided a rhythm of breathing which led most clients into an appropriate experience, into what they could integrate at that moment. The experiences for which Rebirthing became famous—reliving the birth trauma, regression to repressed painful childhood experiences, and retrieving painful memories—still came up, but at a more appropriate rhythm.

Some clients develop "naturally" in therapy: they know instinctively how to do it. These clients advanced better with this new approach. There were, however, other clients for whom the experiences that came up still came up too soon and still were too strong. Although there were no further seriously destabilizing experiences, I was still not satisfied. Even through this new, slowed-down way of working, my clients quickly had dramatic experiences and I continued to have the judgment "Too fast! Too fast!"

The Moment of Grace

I was finishing my doctoral thesis on case histories in the Pali canon, the Buddhist texts whose methods for development I had been studying for many years. You might know how it is possible to study or think about something for a long time, and then suddenly there is a flash of inspiration, a moment of illumination, a moment of grace when finally we see what has been in front of our nose all the time. All of a sudden I noticed the similarity between the methods described in the texts and the methods I was using!

This is what the text says. The Buddha is speaking,

There is one dhamma, *Monks, which when developed and practiced frequently is very fruitful and deserves great praise. What is this one* dhamma? *It is mindfulness of breathing. And how, Monks, is mindfulness of breathing developed? How does it become very fruitful and deserving of great praise when practiced frequently?*

This is how. A monk goes into the forest or to the foot of a tree or to an uninhabited place and sits with his legs crossed, and with his body erect he generates mindfulness and being mindful he breathes in and being mindful he breathes out.

As he breathes in a long breath he recognizes that he is breathing in a long breath; as he breathes out a long breath, he recognizes that he is breathing out a long breath. As he breathes in a short breath he recognizes that he is breathing in a short breath; as he breathes out a short breath, he recognizes that he is breathing out a short breath.

He trains himself to breathe in experiencing his whole body and to breathe out experiencing his whole body. He trains himself to breathe in calming bodily activity and to breathe out calming bodily activity.

He trains himself to breathe in experiencing joy and to breathe out experiencing joy; to breathe in experiencing happiness and to breathe out experiencing happiness.

He trains himself to breathe in experiencing mental activity and to breathe out experiencing mental activity; to breathe in calming mental activity and to breathe out calming mental activity; to breathe in experiencing mind and to breathe out experiencing mind.

He trains himself to breathe in pleasing the mind, and to breathe out pleasing the mind; to breathe in concentrating the mind and to breathe out concentrating the mind; to breathe in releasing the mind and to breathe out releasing the mind.

He trains himself to breathe in observing impermanence and to breathe out observing impermanence; to breathe in observing freedom from passion and to breathe out observing freedom from passion; to breathe in observing cessation and to breathe out observing cessation; to breathe in observing renunciation; to breathe out observing renunciation.[8]

In this text breath is the basis for developmental work, as in Rebirthing, but what is central is observation of the breath without changing or forcing anything. The breath is observed and used as a support for awareness and the cultivation of altered states of consciousness.

Some exercises in the Buddhist texts are based on awareness while others are based on concentration; both may lead to trance states. In Rebirthing, too, there are sessions of pure awareness, sessions of deep concentration and trance states: sessions in which the breathing breathes us and absorbs us into an experience and we cannot pull ourselves out of it until the breath lets us go.

At last I could diagnose the problem. I remembered many experiences in my Rebirthing sessions that had overwhelmed me. Instead of me having these experiences, they had had me: my foundation had been insufficient for integration. This was why I had entered Jungian analysis. I understood that many clients who quickly got into strong and dramatic experiences did not have sufficient means to integrate them.

Inspired by my new understanding of the Buddhist breathing exercises, I decided to start new clients in a comfortable sitting posture rather than lying down, as it is harder to slip into a trance state in a sitting position. I decided, too, only to ask them to observe their breathing, using the following simple instructions, "Put your attention on your breathing and tell me what happens."

This was the solution. I was satisfied and enthusiastic. Results were constructed on the solid foundation of awareness. In working in this way I lost nothing in terms of effective results and I gained greatly in terms of the quality of the development of my clients and my happiness and satisfaction in my work.

That was the birth of what I began to call Gentle Rebirthing.

Conscious Breathing Techniques

It gradually became clear to me that I had developed several different ways of using Conscious Breathing Techniques and a structured way in which to use them. I realized too that not all of these techniques could be called "Rebirthing," and, as I said above, I now formally call the method I use *Conscious Breathing Techniques*. The structure is in six parts. It is not rigid. Stages are not discrete but may flow into each other.

1. Awareness Work with the Breath or Analytical Breathwork

My first step is to teach *awareness work with the breath* or *Analytical Breathwork*. We need first of all to learn awareness in order to work on our Soul Quest. We need to know what we are feeling and thinking if we wish to develop.

New clients take their first sessions sitting comfortably, supported by cushions. I give the instruction, *"Put your attention on your breathing and tell me what happens."* This is all I asked Gordon to do at the beginning of the session with which I opened this chapter.

Some clients can follow this instruction easily, as they have good access to their feelings. They cry or are angry. They remember hurts and injuries and they integrate them. Other clients have no awareness of what is happening either on a physical or on a mental level: they do not feel their emotions, they do not receive their body's messages, and they do not know what they are thinking. They have to learn recognize these things. Various techniques will bring them to this awareness. One is to have them breathe into the different parts of their body and discover what each part is feeling. This anchors them in their body, as breath is a means of grounding. It is something to come back to at any time when experiences become too painful or too intense.

2. Introduction to Independent Breathwork

When clients are aware of what is happening in their mind and body, I introduce Independent Breathwork. The client usually lies on a mattress for this work. I invite them: *"Put your attention on your breathing, let your body provide the rhythm, and tell me what happens."* Nothing is forced or exaggerated. There is no attempt to make the breath larger or smaller, faster or slower, or to change or control it in any way. The body is trusted to regulate the breathing and guide the process. It provides the appropriate rhythm. Sometimes the breath is spontaneously connected, other times it is not. Sometimes the breathing heightens awareness, sometimes it leads to trance. What happens is always appropriate: a repressed experience, thought, or feeling that the client can cope with becomes conscious and is integrated. We can trust Soul to guide our process of development: we do not need to push it or to attack it with violent methods.

Through these two steps—first the awareness work with the breath or Analytical Breathwork and then the introduction to Independent Breathwork—a basis of self-knowledge is built up. Painful experiences are recalled and integrated. Clients learn how to work with and to contain their own process. All of the experiences traditionally connected with Rebirthing, including the famous reliving of the birth trauma, come up through this way of working, if they are ready to be integrated.

3. Introducing Conscious Connected Breathing

After a certain number of sessions, most clients become ready for advanced work. They have a good foundation, good self-awareness, and good self-esteem and are ready to integrate stronger experiences. At this point I invite the client: *"Put your attention on your breathing, let your body provide the rhythm and then, respecting that rhythm, make your breathing connected."* Connected breathing is more likely to lead to trance states although it will not necessarily do so. It will certainly lead to strong experiences and that is why I will only induce it with clients who have already developed a solid foundation. Sometimes I propose this kind of breathing, and then something else happens. The breath guides the process and is a reliable guide, so I never push a client to do something that is not happening naturally. Awareness means accepting what is happening at the moment. Clients who are not ready for this phase will not be able to do connected breathing: their body simply will not let it happen.

4. Working the Breath

What I mean here is *any form and any rhythm* of consciously connected breathing intentionally undertaken and worked strongly like
a physical exercise. For this work there is no regular instruction
that I systematically give to all clients. I will discuss with the client
what our goals are for the session, and related to that I will propose
a rhythm of breathing and perhaps a part of the body in which to
focus the breath. The client and I have an agreement that if what
has been proposed does not take place, we will not try force it, but
rather we will surrender to whatever the breath brings up.

Working the Breath induces intense emotional experiences,
regressions, and higher states of consciousness. When it has been
well-prepared for, it is a way of playing with the breath and having adventures with it. Rebirthing consciously undertaken, in
strength and not through an overwhelming upsurgence of the
unconscious, leads to wonderful experiences. Jennifer experienced healing energy surging through her hands; Zak had the
archetypal experience of himself as a great magician/priest.

5. Advanced Energy Work with the Breath

When we are at ease with our breathing, we use our breath pur-
posefully to clear from our energy-field unproductive thoughts,
habits, and attitudes, unnecessary influences, old relationship
problems and tendencies towards relationship problems, and
energy left over from past-life problems and experiences. This
work is difficult and destabilizing for people with insufficient
experience. *Do not do it yourself before you are prepared, or with a
client who is insufficiently prepared.* That is spiritual materialism.
This is truly advanced energy work.

6. Advanced Awareness Work with the Breath

This is meditation. A client who has reached this stage no
longer needs me. When we are advanced in using our breath as
the basis for our practice of awareness, we can deal with anything
that comes up. We give ourselves Breathwork sessions. We use
our breath to integrate our daily experiences.

Constructive Criticism

Breathwork as practiced in modern therapeutic contexts is a new method and it is exceptionally powerful. If dreams are the royal road to the unconscious, Breathwork is the royal expressway. When a technique is that powerful, and new, it takes time to learn how to use it well. My constructive criticism will concern Traditional Rebirthing, the use of hyperventilation, the choice of suitable clients, claims about healing, literature, professional organization, and Breathwork's limitations.

Traditional Rebirthing

What I noticed with Rebirthing was that there were three types of outcome: (1) people could just do Rebirthing; (2) people protected themselves with tetany; (3) people could not do Rebirthing.

(1) People who can just do Rebirthing.

Traditional Rebirthing works for these rebirthees. They cope with the strong experiences, remain stable, integrate what happens, and make good progress. Many people fall into this category. I consider myself to be among them as I learned so much through Rebirthing.

(2) People who protect themselves with tetany.

Hyperventilation and tetany are part of the mythology of Rebirthing, and all sorts of explanations are put forward to account for them. Rebirthers gathered together around a beer may talk proudly about these painful experiences in a macho fashion—especially the men who have suffered for ten sessions or more. Many Rebirthing books justify hyperventilation and tetany. They argue that Rebirthing is a cure for hyperventilation.[9] There is no medical evidence that I know of to support this claim. *Hyperventilation rapes the unconscious.* It forces into consciousness painful experiences or altered states of consciousness that the client may not be ready to integrate. This accounts for the hysteria frequently present in groups where hyperventilation is practiced. Tetany prevents this rape from taking place. The psychological function of tetany is to prevent material that cannot be integrated from coming up from the unconscious and overwhelming the client: the pain that tetany produces takes all the attention available. Tetany also prevents clients from having experiences their Rebirther cannot cope with: some clients stop having tetany when they change their Rebirther. The unconscious protects through tetany. When there is a good foundation which allows for the integration of painful events, tetany does not happen, even during the strongest connected breathing rhythms.

(3) People who could not do Rebirthing.

Rebirthing brings up extreme experiences: traumatic memories, ecstatic and other altered states of consciousness. When the foundation of personal knowledge and development is insufficient for the integration of these experiences, various problems ensue. A strong Aikido teacher of about thirty had an overwhelming ecstatic experience—a *Kundalini* awakening—in his first Rebirthing session. As he had no base into which to integrate this experience, it so terrified him that he stopped Rebirthing, judging it to be too dangerous.

The strong ecstatic experiences can cause people to become flippy. Then they may take up various types of rather odd religious beliefs or other types of unrealistic beliefs, or fall into superstitious thought (Albery, p. 68f and elsewhere), or follow gurus,[10] or even like Leonard Orr who invented Rebirthing proclaim themselves a guru. Orr now calls himself "Young Len Orr Raja," and explains, "The guru game when played consciously by both the guru and the devotee is a beautiful game." He invites us to become his disciples on condition that "you have to maintain economic self-sufficiency and tithe to me." (*Breathe*, Issue No. 58.) Another teacher of breathing and other energy methods permits his students (or are they, too, disciples?) to call him "Buddha"! When we have a good foundation including a strong sense of who we are and a good basis of knowledge, we are aware of our natural potential for altered states of consciousness and we are able to integrate these when they occur. People without this basis identify with these states and become caught up in a fantasy about their own specialness. They project these experiences onto external sources—gurus or grandiose ideas—seeking authentication for their specialness in this way. Jung called this inflation—being blown up! Inflation is a sign that one is following the Ego Quest. Inflation is, of course, not limited to Rebirthers.

Many Rebirthers, like the practitioners of the Tao in ancient times,[11] are committed to the achievement of Physical Immortality. Believing in physical immortality as an achievable goal and being willing to teach this belief to clients can be a prerequisite if one wishes to become a member of some Rebirthing schools.

These were the three kinds of outcome that I noticed with Traditional Rebirthing. These outcomes are not mutually exclusive. Many rebirthees will go beyond tetany after a number of sessions and be able to open up to and integrate the material that comes up. Many rebirthees who have spent some time being unrealistic acquire a foundation and become realistic. The commitment to Physical Immortality often changes with time to a commitment to a healthy and long life.

The Use of Hyperventilation

It is normal in all Breathwork sessions that breathing rhythms change. The breath may become faster or slower, stronger or weaker, heavier or lighter, with long pauses between in- and out-breath, or connected, and so forth. Certain experiences evoke particular breathing rhythms. Even if I begin a session asking only that the client put his or her attention on the breathing (Part 1 of the structure), breathing rhythms will change in function with what the client is experiencing and feeling. When a client is working through the birth trauma, for example, rapid connected breathing often happens spontaneously. Augmented breathing is characteristic of some spontaneous shamanic experiences.

Hyperventilation induced by the therapist, and augmented breathing rhythms provided naturally by the body are quite separate phenomena and it is misleading to call them by the same name. Hyperventilation is uncontrolled and uncontrollable rapid upper chest breathing and is a characteristic of panic attacks and other serious problems. It is a medical problem.[12] Rebirthers and other breathworkers should be cautious about working with clients who suffer from it. I am against getting clients to hyperventilate.

Augmented breathing rhythms happen normally in everyday life: during or after exercise, for example, or when we are frightened, or during sex. In these circumstances they are *normal.* When they occur of themselves in a therapeutic situation, they are no less normal. Augmented breathing rhythms happen naturally in various ways and for various reasons in different types of Conscious Breathing sessions. Rebirthers and other breathworkers can justifiably ask a client to take a larger in-breath—in the sense of taking a bit more life and energy to work with. For clients who cannot feel their emotions, this is a good technique.

My friend and colleague Wilfried Ehrmann, who runs the ATMAN-Project, a training for professional Breathworkers in Austria, agrees "that hyperventilation should not be a goal in a breathing session," and that "rebirthing is not about sensations, and pushing the breathing does not lead anywhere." Wilfried has supplied me with two case histories of "sessions where hyperventilation came by itself, brought about by the letting go of control," and where "the rebirther could only have stopped this natural flow in order to prevent the hyperventilation syndrome." Here they are in Wilfried's own words:

"Burt had great difficulties in opening up to his emotions and to his body in a group. His first session was without any depth, shallow relaxation. In his second session he dared to breathe more and got into hyperventilation. And that helped him to feel himself.

"Max is a very timid guy who describes himself as weak, dependent, sensitive, and with many problems in life. In his first breathing sessions he soon came to a deeper yet controlled breathing rhythm. Encouraged by music, he let go of the exhale at one point and the breathing got very strong and intense, which led him into tetany. It was easy to help him relax and open up to a very subtle energy flow. Afterwards he said his most important insight was that he had to go for it in his life wherever he felt like quitting and avoiding."

I quote Wilfried further: "I have more examples which indicate to me that for some people it is very important to experience symptoms of hyperventilation in their process of self-discovery by breathing. Often it is the gateway to deeper feelings, like a bridge which can be left behind once the door is open. Some people need to go the rough way in order to find the smooth and gentle realms. I often get a feeling in the beginning, when someone starts to breathe, that he/she will go into hyperventilation as if his/her body would have decided to do that.

"Other people's ways are different. Everyone is unique. But why exclude a phenomenon which is brought up by the breath out of its "natural" process? (By natural I do not mean according to the inborn nature of man; I use this word in the sense of not manipulated, not pushed, not intended by the rebirther out of some concept.) Of course hyperventilation should be overcome as soon as possible, as it is usually an unpleasant feeling. Something goes wrong when a person still hyperventilates in the twentieth session. The teaching should aim at the relaxation of the exhale and, in fact, I do not know anybody who did not learn that after a few sessions.

". . . I see hyperventilation as a quite sophisticated tool of the unconscious to trick the permanent manipulation and control of consciousness." (Personal communication, 17 October, 1995.)

In a new method, like Conscious Breathing Techniques, we still have to seek definitions and terminology. Wilfried Ehrmann and I are talking about the same thing, except that he uses the term *hyperventilation* and I would like to reserve that term for the medical breathing problem and use *augmented breathing rhythms* for what the breath and the body do naturally in Breathwork. Wilfried and I agree that this should not be "manipulated, pushed or intended by the rebirther."

Suitable Clients

As in all of the new therapies, and many traditional ones, client suitability is a problem and there is no easy answer. There is an excellent discussion of this problem in Richard Mowbray's very important book, *The Case against Psychotherapy Registration*. On the subject of client suitability for human potential work, he says,

> . . . *it is a necessary precondition for human potential work that clients have* Sufficient Available Functioning Adult Autonomy (SAFAA). *At and beyond this level of functioning,* healing *could be said to become* "wholing" *and it is to this that human potential work addresses itself. (p.183)*

Human potential work is another way of talking about the Soul Quest, and this seems to me a very adequate precondition.

Not everyone is a suitable client for any technique. Some people need to spend time doing some form of analysis or Gestalt before they start a method as direct as Conscious Breathing. Others do well starting with Conscious Breathing and then after that they may get more benefit from analysis or Gestalt.

Claims about Healing

The early books about Rebirthing tend to make extravagant claims for healing which, to the best of my knowledge, are unsupported. As I said at the beginning of this chapter, seeking for physical healing can be a form of spiritual materialism. Trying to prove that any particular method heals physical ailments is spurious too. There are cases of healing claimed for, or attributed to, all of the methods I have ever heard of. There is certainly no new method that does not claim this.

Literature

Literature used to be a problem. The early books about Rebirthing tend to be a bit wacky and to make semi-miraculous if not quite miraculous claims. I find that a part of their charm. Read, enjoy, use your common sense, and be discerning.

Unfortunately, too many new books only repeat what the earlier books said, and this is very tiresome.

Fortunately, there are ever more good books about Breathwork being published. I have given what I hope is a comprehensive bibliography. Read, become informed, and be discerning.

Professional Organization

The International Breathwork Foundation[13] was established in 1994 to provide information, encourage research, and support the professionalism of practitioners and trainings. It holds an annual conference which is highly international and is appropriately called *Global Inspiration*.

Limits to Breathwork

In my own work as a therapist, I have not yet discovered the limits to what I and my clients can do when working consciously and intelligently with the breath. People who work with the breath are only at the beginning of a most exciting time in their discipline. I am very enthusiastic about what I have discovered so far. I have written about it briefly here, but I consider the results so important that I will be writing a book on this subject.

The Path of the Soul is the Breath

Breath is life: without breath there is no life. Our breathing *is* our state of consciousness. Our habitual rhythms of breathing regulate our state of consciousness and our emotions in daily life: a change in our rhythm of breathing induces a change in our state of consciousness. Breath is life and life is Relationship. The physical act of breathing in and out—taking, receiving, holding on, holding out, giving and letting go—symbolizes relating. Love, communication, attention, respect, money, food, and sex all contain these processes. Concentration on the breath develops awareness: awareness liberates the breath. When the breath is free, life is free. Through working with the breath, we can resolve problems whatever their origination: conception, birth, childhood, adult life, or past lives. Our breath brings us gently to the innermost depths of our being. It lifts us into altered states of consciousness.

Soul-Questing is normal. Like a river to the ocean, like a bird that instinctively knows its migration route, the Soul Path finds its own way. Soul knows its path of development. Soul is neither to be forced nor directed: this disturbs its process. Soul is to be followed. Soul leads us to Soul-level.

TWENTY-ONE
Voice Dialogue

The inventors of Voice Dialogue are Hal and Sidra Stone (Winkelman). He was originally trained as a Jungian analyst and she is a psychotherapist. I fell in love with this technique at my first encounter with it, and took to it as a duck to water. The first book about it, *Embracing Our Selves: Voice Dialogue Manual*, made sense immediately and I was able to give good sessions after having received only one! Lots of people have this experience: there seem to be many people who are "naturals" for this technique. I think this is because it is so simple and so truthful.

Voice Dialogue takes us into the drama that is our personality. We talk with the players who are our different subpersonalities, "Voices," or energies—the different roles we play. Before we become aware of them, they possess and control us. As we dialogue with them, we recognize their function in our personality, and learn to respect and honor them and their work.

Our personality is our riches; the number and variety of our subpersonalities is endless. Some of these are the archetypal roles played in the family, parental roles like the good and bad father or mother; the nourishing mother or father; the rejecting, angry, or rational parent. Some are child roles; our Vulnerable, Rebellious, Happy, Sad, Playful, and other child-selves. Some are almost caricatures of behavior: the Inner Critic, who is devoted to criticizing ourselves and others; the Perfectionist, who never fails to inform us that neither we nor anyone else does things well enough; the Pusher, who, insatiable, tells us we have never done enough; the Protector-Controller, directing the players and the game, or trying to. We have other archetypal energies, including mythological and astrological ones, available to support us.

Sometimes quite different energy appears. The client's posture changes. Her body stands differently, moves differently, speaks differently—empowered beyond doubting. The air vibrates differently. The facilitator feels awe. Soul manifests, not as a subpersonality but as a Super-personality.

Some Voice Dialogue Sessions

The room that Voice Dialogue sessions take place in is also a theater setting. Voice Dialogue is the play that is our character with our various parts or subpersonalities as the actors. In this theaterpiece the client plays all the roles except one: that of facilitator. Sessions begin with client and facilitator sitting opposite each other on chairs. When the client is in that position, the rule is that they are "themselves," not identified with any role, in the ideal state that according to the theory is the Aware Ego. No other subpersonality may take up exactly that position.

My role as facilitator is to help clients enter into the energy of one or several subpersonalities. Each subpersonality or Voice is treated as a distinct individual—within the framework of the piece of theater. I ask the Voices questions, discover their names, ideas, ideals, and constructive or destructive functions and purposes within the personality of the client. I listen. I draw them out. I am accepting. I am never judgmental. One of my clients called Voice Dialogue a serious game.

Clients often are afraid that they will not be able to "do" Voice Dialogue, but this never happens and they are always surprised how easy it is. I interview the client and note which energies are most present. Then I ask which of these s/he would like me to talk to. When s/he has chosen, I say, "Find the place in the room where you feel the energy of that Voice most strongly," and the dialogue begins.

At the end of a session, I ask the client to sit next to me, and I review the session. In this position the client is the witness to my account and to my physical view of the session. Clients may not comment from this position, but after my summary, they return to the position of the Aware Ego from which they started and we discuss and integrate what was learned. On both sides, our Aware Ego keeps in balance the influence of our subpersonalities.

Voice Dialogue can be done with the elements of a dream or a work of art or a fairy story, as well as with our subpersonalities.

A description of some Voice Dialogue sessions will give you an impression of the power of this technique.

Rosanne came for what was to be her third or fourth Conscious Breathing session. She is about thirty. She sat on the sofa like a rebellious adolescent. Rebellious energy is not inclined to accept suggestions. The challenge in front of me was to make an ally out of that energy. Rosanne and I had not yet tried Voice Dialogue. I proposed that we do something new, something like theater. I hoped that a Rebel subpersonality would agree to play a game. It would very likely refuse to work. Rosanne agreed. The Rebel told about herself. This subpersonality gave Rosanne the strength to overcome the horrible suffering of being sexually abused by her father during her early childhood. It supported her intelligence and gave her courage to believe in herself. Through Voice Dialogue, Rosanne discovered the aspect of her character that would not define her as a "Victim"—that rebelled against the fact that she was a victim. Once this Voice had expressed itself, Rosanne's energy changed and a different subpersonality manifested, soft and feminine. For a woman who has been abused as a child, everything connected with the feminine is wounded and being feminine is in itself dangerous. The emergence of this subpersonality who is the "Woman" in Rosanne was very healing.

Brenda was experienced in Conscious Breathing Techniques and Voice Dialogue. She had to make a difficult and important decision. We dialogued with a Voice that wanted to decide "yes," with a Voice that wanted to decide "no," and with a Voice that wanted to avoid making a decision. Then a new subpersonality introduced itself, "I'm the one who makes the decisions here. I am the Manager. I let the others talk, I listen to them because it is necessary to listen, it is respectful and right. I listen to them. I discuss with them. I weigh up what they say, and on this basis I make decisions." Technically this subpersonality is called the Protector-Controller. Often this subpersonality is rigid, inflexible, and on the defensive, intent on protecting the status quo of the personality and obstructing change. In the present case, however, it was a gifted Manager: wise, capable, compassionate, ideal to have in any business. Brenda made a good decision.

Ronald is an enterprising young man in his early twenties. He was no longer a boy but not quite fully a man. He had started a new business when many people of his age have problems finding employment. He was confident and modest at the same time, which gave him a lot of charm. Ronald knew he had something to do in his life but he did not know quite what. I asked to speak to the part of him that was about thirty years old. Ronald-the-boy changed into Ronald-the-man. This more mature part began to talk. Ronald-the-man had many useful things to say to Ronald-the-boy.

Sheila dreamed of a train that was going through the mountains. The engine at the front of the train, the central part, and the rear carriage were all clear elements in her dream, as were the mountains, and a village in them. We dialogued with each of these elements. It turned out that the engine was the part of her that wanted to go forward and achieve things, and that it was in conflict with the last carriage, the part of her that wanted nothing to change but felt pulled along.

Voice Dialogue respects energy and opposite energies. Where there is a Saint in a personality, there is also a Sinner! Ralph has a very strong Controller. He is always preoccupied with how Ralph presents himself and concerned about the impression Ralph makes. This Controller was determined to control my thoughts about Ralph—or rather, the thoughts he *imagined* that I had. Ralph asked me to talk to "the part of him that loved women." Ralph is a rather theatrical fellow and became ever more sanctimonious as this Voice continued. When it had finished he looked particularly self-satisfied. I took him off his guard and surprised him with the question, "Can I talk to the part of you that hates women?" After a moment, Ralph fell about laughing and we laughed together. He got the point.

I get a great deal of pleasure from using this technique. It is fun to use, and I feel moved and privileged to share the revealing Soul-level moments it inevitably gives rise to.

Constructive Criticism

Conscious Breathing is my first technique—the one I use most frequently and am most involved with. I use Voice Dialogue as a supporting technique. This is also how its creators describe it. My constructive criticism will concern the literature and professional organization, the limitations of practitioners, client suitability, Voice Dialogue and channeling, and energy awareness.

Literature and Professional Organization

There are quite excellent books about Voice Dialogue written by its inventors, Hal and Sidra Stone.The books are a source of inspiration and I encourage you to read them. The basic idea is easy to understand and the technique is simply explained. A good critical literature exists too and sets this technique in context. Its inventors take a constructively critical approach to their own technique[14] and are constantly refining it. There is a newsletter called *Voice Dialogue International.*[15]

There is no professional organization. Hal and Sidra teach their technique but do not certify practitioners. They see Voice Dialogue as an adjunct to other techniques, and I agree with this view.

The Limitations of the Practitioner

As with any other technique, the limitations of Voice Dialogue are those of the practitioner. Eveline was in love with her Inner Child Voices and spent many sessions having her facilitator talk with them. The only ones she was willing to talk to, however, were the "good" Inner Children. Eveline had a very powerful Selfish Inner Child. Unfortunately her various facilitators were not aware of it, so it never got spoken to. Eveline is stuck in the Ego Quest. Sadly, she wants to hold on to her illusions about herself, not trusting that what she will discover when she lets them go will be much better. She is not courageous enough to meet her Shadow, and invariably chooses facilitators with similar limitations. However much we may love one or another of our Voices, we have to surrender this attachment in order to progress on our Soul Quest. Some of the Voices we wish to meet least of all when we function on the Ego-level are our best helpers towards Soul-level.

Facilitators who are in the grip of their Inner Children will be preoccupied with yours at the expense of the development of your Adult Voices, and you need competent adult subpersonalities in order to live a competent adult life. Facilitators who are defending Controllers of all kinds are in the grip of their Controller: they will want to control your process and direct your development rather than to accompany you as you follow your Soul Path.

Voice Dialogue can be abused as a way to avoid responsibility by attributing our behavior to one or another of our Voices. Marsha has a good knowledge of the Voice Dialogue technique and herself facilitates sessions. Marsha expressed how she was feeling in the Voice Dialogue idiom, "I have been feeling afraid. I looked to see what it could come from and I discovered a Frightened Child to which I became the Mother and I took this child into my heart." The words sounded very beautiful and poetic, but the expression on her face told a different story. "Did the fear then go away?" I asked her. Marsha answered, a little sheepishly and with fear in her Voice, "No." I call this *the Voices trap*. Our strong feelings, emotions, and instincts belong to us and not to external Voices. We use the metaphor of subpersonalities or Voices to understand our behavior and then we integrate what we have learned into our wholeness.

Practitioners can also be inspiring and extend a technique. One of the graduates from my school uses Voice Dialogue for birth trauma work very successfully.

Suitable Clients

Voice Dialogue, like any of the new therapies, should not be done with anyone who does not have Sufficient Available Functioning Adult Autonomy (see page 172). Voice Dialogue can cause clients to experience their character as fragmented. To talk to subpersonalities is to work within a metaphor. We project our subpersonalities into Voices to become aware of influences upon us, and then it is our task to take back these projections and integrate them into a whole and healed self. We need to be clear that we are, in fact, one person, one character with many facets. In a person without a center to their personality and without a sufficiently strong sense of identity, distributing behaviors to subpersonalities can bring about further fragmentation.

Voice Dialogue and Channeling

These days many people are hearing Voices. They claim that the Voices belong to external entities, dead relatives, or spirit guides. Sometimes these entities wish to talk through the person, and the person becomes channel. People have visions too. Hearing Voices and having visions can be truly uplifting experiences that serve our Soul Quest, but they can also be rather dubious Ego-serving experiences. Many people use channeling to boost their self-esteem, claiming authority and trust for the information because it comes from an outside source. There is a tendency to give more credence to an untestable source than to living people who can respond to questions.

Much of what is channeled is either common sense or harmless, but a certain amount is harmful, full of messages of doom and destruction that lead people into various forms of misery including foolish behavior, inflation, and spiritual materialism. "Channels" make grandiose claims about the "beings" they are channeling and start sects. Sects are disempowering. With a wise Voice Dialogue facilitator, and under appropriate circumstances, Voices that claim to belong to external entities can be dialogued with. Visions can be worked with in the same way as dreams. This way we can discern whether what we are experiencing is wholesome or not. We can find out whether these Voices are our Inner Critic in disguise or some form of Ego-inspired self-seeking or whether they indeed serve our Soul Quest. However much we love our Voices and visions, if we are not willing to test their value, we are following an Ego Quest and not a Soul Quest.

Awareness and Energy Awareness

Voice Dialogue is an excellent means for training awareness in general and energy awareness in particular. We hear our different subpersonalities or Voices speak and we notice how unmistakably different our voice sounds with each one. We notice too that our body feels and moves differently with each of our different Voices. It feels lighter or heavier, taller or smaller, masculine or feminine, young or old, depending on the particular Voice. Our breath too may flow more easily or be blocked, depending on the Voice. Voice Dialogue is a basic Energy Psychotherapy technique.

I end this chapter with a paragraph from a letter from Hal Stone:

It is important to realize that this work is not about Voice Dialogue. Voice Dialogue is simply a vehicle for accomplishing what needs to be accomplished. This work is about the Aware Ego. It is about standing between opposites and having energetic mastery between the various opposites. Only in this way can the unconscious do its proper work and begin to manifest as the teacher it was meant to be.

Awareness is a relatively easy state to ignite and its flame is relatively difficult to blow out. The Aware Ego is difficult to ignite and its flame blows out very easily and with amazing regularity. It is important to see Voice Dialogue in its proper perspective, a method for activating the Aware Ego and hence the deeper intelligence of the unconscious psyche.
                    —(Personal communication, 11 December, 1995.)

TWENTY-TWO
Past-Life Therapy

Conscious Breathing Techniques and Voice Dialogue often naturally and effortlessly lead into Past-life work, or Reincarnation or Regression Therapy as it is also called.

Some people have no doubt about the reality of past human lives, others are uncertain, while still others think that we live only once. What is my position? I have had access to human and animal past-life memories since my earliest teens. As a small child I had contact with non-human memories. In the course of my Soul Quest, my past-life work took me into deeper dimensions and these became clear. When I remember past-life incidents, it is with the same intensity and quality as childhood memories or memories of yesterday's experiences.

Past-life memories, like memories of childhood, come back "inexplicably" on our Soul Path. They reveal themselves. Whenever this has happened to me, it has invariably been of the greatest importance on my Soul Quest. I have visions (as do many other people), and these too have the same quality of reality for me as my everyday life. I go in and out of my body and always have. I had to learn that other people did not necessarily do so.

Soul and psyche are complex. We live our life, but we also live in relationship to life, searching for its meaning, interpreting events, and trying to make sense of our experiences. We have ordinary consciousness and altered states of consciousness. Soul

184

guides and teaches us in so many different ways: through present life experiences, through relationships, through symbols, through visions, through suffering. Part of my discipline of being as surrendered to Soul as I can be is to keep my views flexible. I do not want to be dogmatic. I do not want to impose my beliefs on my clients. That is unfair. It is each client's Soul Quest task to decide in which way to understand the material that comes up in our sessions, and mine to accept their interpretations with the proviso that the work is grounded and that common sense and good sense prevail.

Some Past-Life Sessions

Most past-life sessions are much like present-life sessions, except that they take place in costume and in historical settings. They deal with the usual human problems: family, relationships, work, sex, health, pain and suffering, and the problem of trying to make sense of life. Usually a past-life session helps us to explain attitudes that make no sense in the context of this life alone. Roger Woolger, in his seminal book on past lives, *Other Lives, Other Selves*, has pointed out that most past-life work is not based on lifetimes in which we are important and influential people, but where we are ordinary people, living ordinary lives.

Whenever we cannot integrate a traumatic event, whether in this or in a past life, it influences our present life. When past-life traumatic events are not integrated, they influence the lives that follow. A young man gets killed in battle. There was no time to live the life he hoped for. A beloved wife and young children are left behind. He can now do nothing to protect or to provide for them. Some lives later he is called Arnie and comes for therapy. Arnie wonders why he is quite unable to take up an excellent job offer that would require traveling. He wonders why he cannot sleep each time his wife takes the children to visit her parents for a few days. Through past-life work he remembers that significant previous life, and his dying thought which was "I should never have left my family." This thought works like a post-hypnotic suggestion, as do all of our beliefs, and prevents him from leaving his family today. Arnie integrates those elements from his past life which are controlling his present life, and takes the job.

Not all past-life work has to do with healing physical trauma. Elaine was preoccupied with being loving. She is a truly loving, giving, generous, warm-hearted person, who is always asking herself whether she could not be more loving and caring. She remembered that in a previous life, during a famine, when she was rich and well-provided for, she had closed her doors to the poor. In reality there had been too many of them for her to care for. She, however, had never forgiven herself and was continually trying to make up for it. She married a series of men she had to provide for, took on good causes, and worked very hard for very little in order to improve the lot of disadvantaged people.

Past-life work has many dimensions. Some past-life sessions are not at all like present-life sessions. Clients remember lives on other planets and in other universes. Sometimes they are incarnate here on Earth in human form for the first time and find it very confusing. Occupying a human body is new and strange and difficult. Social life is a problem: they don't know the rules and cannot make out what is expected of them. They are more cooperative and willing than others who are familiar with the rules. They would like to "get it right" and don't know how to. These new people have to learn the basics, the most elementary aspects of life on Earth, and it is very hard for them. Graham said, "I come from somewhere else. You can call it Mars but it is not the actual planet Mars. I feel so lost. Please, can you tell me some of the rules here?" He needed to be told what childhood was, what adolescence was, why an education was necessary, and about jobs and relationships.

There are others who come from different time-spaces. They have had many reincarnations on Earth and know very well through past experience what life here is like. They are the Masters. They come out of their immense compassion for humankind to improve life here and to support the Soul Quest.

Their commitment to Soul is unconditional. It is not for me to tell any part of their stories. They do so themselves when they are ready.

Constructive Criticism

There is an ever-growing literature about past-life therapy. There are various schools, but no general professional organization to control standards and practitioners or the use of particular techniques. My particular constructive criticism of past-life therapy here will concern the issue of whether past lives really exist, good and bad techniques in past-life work, and when past-life therapy is or is not appropriate. The problem of client suitability is the same as for Conscious Breathing Techniques and Voice Dialogue.

Do Past Lives Exist?

Do past lives really exist? Do we all have a sequence of incarnations? Some religions take this for granted; others are more discrete or may, in their public and organized form, deny past lives. Nevertheless, some acceptance of the reality of past lives can be found in the esoteric teachings of all religions.

Soul communicates in many different ways. Is a memory of a past life an occasion where previously unconscious experience is becoming conscious, or is it to be taken symbolically? Much past-life work seems to be related to real experiences. I gave a few examples above of some sessions that convinced me. Some past-life work, however, seems to be a symbolic way of working through present problems that are too overwhelming or too painful to work with directly. Frank remembered a past life in which he had been mean and tyrannical. At that time it would have been too confronting for him to accept any relationship between that life and his present behavior. Some time later he was able to integrate that in his present life he was behaving no differently! Had the past life really taken place? I had my doubts. It was easier for him to become conscious and self-responsible for how he was conducting his present life through a symbolic representation.

Good and Bad Techniques in Past-Life Work

Sometimes past lives come up naturally and spontaneously in Conscious Breathing or Voice Dialogue sessions, and that is my preferred method. Then there is no induction, and techniques for working with the material are no different from those usually used in these sessions.

Sometimes it is necessary to help a client into a past life through an induction. Clifford had permanent neck-ache. He had been to doctors and osteopaths and knew that there was no physical problem. My hypothesis was that the neck-ache was likely to be connected either to his birth-trauma—perhaps a cord around the neck or a clumsy delivery—or to a past life. I asked Clifford to really feel his neck-ache, and to let the feeling get stronger. He started to squirm, pushing his head back. I asked, "What's happening?" "They've caught me and they're strangling me," he answered. "Where are you?" I asked. He was in a prison. Then I understood that we were dealing with past-life material, and continued the session in the appropriate way. The simple technique of asking the right question at the right time brings up appropriate material in all types of therapy, using the minimum of suggestion.

I try to avoid inductions, and when I do use them to avoid suggestion as much as possible. Induction is very close to hypnotic suggestion and many past-life therapists do indeed use hypnosis. Hypnosis has come into disrepute again, despite the efforts of Neuro-Linguistic practitioners and others to save it, because it is increasingly shown that clients who are hypnotized or deeply relaxed will produce the information that pleases their therapists, whether this is information about sexual or ritual abuse, or about alien abductions. The training of the hypnotist, whether medical or otherwise, seems to make little difference. If you have learned about your past lives through hypnosis, don't forget to use your discernment and common sense, and beware of spiritual materialism.

There are past-life therapists who are into paraphernalia: headphones, suggestive music, darkened rooms, special chairs or beds to lie down on, and so forth. This kind of induction has no simplicity about it and is full of abracadabra and hocus-pocus! These preparations seem intended to flip clients out rather than to ground them. Past-life experiences evoked in this way do not convince me at all.

The Limitations of Practitioners

Much too much past-life work is a marriage between the spiritual materialism of the therapist and the spiritual materialism of the client. Both do the work because they think it makes them more interesting. The therapist's training has been exclusively in regressing people and in being regressed. It does not include relationship, communication or basic therapy skills, or anything else connected with dealing well in the present with our present life or anything related to common sense. Usually there is a smattering of various techniques of suggestion taught, but nothing to professional level. When past-life therapists accept for past-life work clients who have done no therapy before, who have no grounding, whose awareness skills are undeveloped, and who have not begun to deal with this present life's problems, then I have no faith whatever in the results.

Some past-life therapists have addictions. One discovers that all of their clients have been sexually abused, or have been through a particular war or a particular period in history, or that they all have something else in common. I cannot believe in past-life work done in these conditions. Rather, these are cases of clients who try to please their therapists by producing what the therapists need. It is a good idea to find out if your past-life therapist has a speciality. If you find your case conforms to that, dare to treat the results with the right amount of doubt.

In all good therapy there are moments of high drama. Integration requires the intense feeling of emotions and the intense remembering of unpleasant experiences so that we recognize what we have suffered. Some past-life therapists particularly love the drama. Then I wonder whether the drama really belongs to the client's experience, or whether the client is fulfilling the therapist's need for drama. Some past-life therapists love the fighting—they are at their happiest when the client is going through some violent incident, kicking, hitting a cushion, yelling and crying. Then it is possible that clients go through past life after past life—or invented past lives—working through the same type of problem to please the unspoken needs of their therapist. This kind of work carries the risk that unpleasant physical feelings, emotional and other fears, and bad experiences in general get reinforced in the present. Instead of integrating the fear of drowning, for example, the client "acts out" with drama, violence, and struggle through any number of drowning incidents, and reinforces the fear of water they came to get rid of. Acting out can be a way of escaping from feelings, especially from vulnerability. Finally the vulnerability will have to be faced, the fear will have to be integrated.

When doing past-life therapy, it is of the utmost importance to thoroughly bring clients back into the present at the end of the session so that they are really clear about who they are, where they live, and what period of history they are in. Not to do this is cruel and irresponsible. I have worked with people after they have been the victims of past-life "cowboys." Meg experienced a life where she was a prostitute. She had not been brought back properly to the present, and so was uncertain of her identity and profession. It does not matter whether her "past life" as a prostitute was real or not; what matters is that she thought she was still in it. It did her marriage and her family no good.

When is Past-Life Therapy Appropriate?

I am often asked to do past-life work. I do not always agree. I will not do it with clients who are not grounded or with clients who do not have enough awareness to do competent Conscious Breathing sessions. Past-life work can too easily be confused with imagination, wishful thinking, and spiritual materialism.

What about people who want to do past-life work just out of curiosity? I am not against that, but my induction would be to discover more about this curiosity, for instance: "Feel your curiosity. Now let it become ever more intense. When you can almost bear it no longer, tell me where you are and what is happening." That could be fun.

There are good reasons for doing past-life work. When it happens of its own, then obviously it requires to be worked with. When no reason for the clients' problems can be found in the present life, it is fruitful to be open to past-life work. And I accept "curiosity" as a reason.

Past-life work is a marvelous testing ground for spiritual materialists. Are we undertaking past-life work as part of our Soul Quest or to serve our Ego Quest? Are we trying to understand who we are and how we became that way, or are we trying to convince ourselves that we are important? Are we seeking to become more self-responsible, or are we seeking through drama and fighting excuses for how we are and for people to blame?

Ego loves paraphernalia, drama, and specialness. Soul is simple. How are you doing your past-life work? Ego-fashion or Soul-fashion?

I consider past-life work important and I enjoy doing it. It is especially profound when a person has developed good awareness and has done a lot of basic work on present-life issues and problems. Then past-life sessions are pure Soul Path, and take clients deeply into their Soul Quest. Having easy access to my past lives has helped me throughout my life to understand who I am and how I function. It has often helped me to understand my relationships with my family and others. Recent past-life work made it possible for me to write this book.

PART 5 FIVE

Ego-Level and Soul-Level

Some people walk the Soul Path through their very nature and cannot do otherwise. They are born strongly and consciously connected to Soul. Soul-Questing is natural for them, and anything else is unnatural and even impossible. Others only have to be given the slightest indication, and they get it: they recognize Soul-level and dedicate their lives to living that way. And there are others whose connection to Soul remains unconscious and who are limited to living on Ego-level. Some people take individual sessions or enter groups or participate in workshops that offer only Ego Therapy and have the capacity to transform what they are receiving into Soul Therapy. Others are offered Soul Therapy, and meet and work with people on Soul-level, but sadly, are unable to receive it because they can only function on Ego-level. How can this be?

Sometimes I am asked, timidly, "Has everyone got a Soul Path? Can everyone develop? Is everyone capable of pursuing the Soul Quest?" We do so desperately want our suffering to come to an end and to be able to enjoy our lives. In our imagination, development leads to permanent happiness. The idea of being unable to succeed in the Soul Quest is frightening. It means that we will be locked into our suffering for the whole of our lives, prisoners of our conditioning and our suffering.

People fail all the time.

Celia was in a training. She thrived for a while, grateful to be with a group of people who could accept and love her. At first she was fearful, as people are when they do something new, and very keen to "get it right." Her gratitude made her modest and she worked hard. As she grew in strength, however, the feeling of inferiority from which she suffered at the beginning became a sense of superiority. She became hostile and aggressive and was unconscious of what she was doing. Her intelligence and her worry about the years she had spent in unsuccessful therapy were not enough. She walked out. Celia did not succeed, as, to her desperate unhappiness, she had not succeeded during ten years of therapy with various therapists. Why not? One could say because she would not cultivate the necessary foundations, or because she would not be honest enough with herself, but that is simplistic. Celia was trying. She did not "not cultivate" any qualities or attitudes out of choice: she *could* not cultivate them. Something in her obstructed her progress.

Juliette complained that other people were manipulative: her mother, her husband, her employer, her colleagues. Juliette is intelligent, sensitive, intuitive, and kind. She is also a selfish, fragile, and manipulative young woman. I concentrated on building her self-esteem: her recognition of her own real value. Only when we have begun to love and to feel compassion for ourselves are we able to integrate our shadow and accept our failings; otherwise our ego is in danger of disintegration. I waited for Juliette to recognize that she was projecting her own manipulativeness onto everyone else. Suddenly Juliette wrote to say that she would stop coming to sessions because I was manipulative. I was now part of that group of everyone except herself! The manipulations are only one facet of Juliette's personality; fundamentally she is truly honest. If she became aware that she manipulated she would be terribly upset and she would stop. Juliette went through the same process with her next therapist.

People succeed all the time, too.

Steve was a typical mother's boy: the son of an adoring, devoted, possessive mother. His body was flabby, lacking in a center and lacking in definition. He made me think of a big puddle of water. From the middle of this puddle gurgled a voice, "I know I am special. I know I have something to do in this world." "Maybe you have and maybe you haven't," I thought, convinced on principle and through discipline—my long experience has taught me that clients know themselves better than I will ever know them—rather than belief. He has. Steve applied himself to his Soul Quest with the deepest commitment, never making a compromise, always accepting the next challenge and going for it. He is no longer a puddle of water: he is strong, decisive, imaginative, creative, and successful.

Mary was interested in everything superstitious. She liked the manipulative power that comes from clairvoyance; her speciality was telling fortunes through cards. She was aware enough to be uneasy with this tendency and undertook a training with the purpose of finding a better way. Mary discovered that she has healing energy in her hands. She is now a source of healing for others, using this energy in a pure and selfless way.

These are typical of the stories of people who succeed. They know that they have something to give to the world and they are determined to discover what this something is and to give it. They work at their Soul Quest. They take individual sessions regularly, follow well-chosen workshops, develop the necessary foundations, and read the necessary books. They do not make compromises and they do not look for short-cuts.

Have these people worked harder than those who have failed? I don't know.

Some people succeed and some people fail. Some of the people who fail are demonstrably unwilling to be self-responsible, but not all of them. Some people fail although they are trying with all of their will. Why do these people fail? The key is Ethics.

Ethics

Soul knows it has something to give to the world; Ego's goal is to get something out of it. What we have first and foremost to give to the world is our ethical behavior. Everything else follows from that. The *guarantee* for success in following the Soul Path is Ethics. Ethics separates the Ego Quest from the Soul Quest.

There is no compromising with Ethics, no negotiating, no philosophizing about the finer points. We either intend not to be harmful to others or we do not have this intention. We either are careful in thought, word, and deed or we are careless. Either we are following the commandments or the code of conduct, or we do not have this intention. Either it is our discipline to be self-responsible, or it is not. And the criteria is so simple: either we are working to take back our projections all of the time, or we are not. That is what it amounts to, and that is an easy way to discern whether we are following a Soul Quest or an Ego Quest. The two are mutually exclusive. The Soul Quest does not demand that we are perfect. It does demand that we have the right intentions. Celia and Juliette in the examples above were just not ethical enough. Celia did not inhibit her aggression and was not careful enough about hurting others, while Juliette was not self-responsible enough but lost herself in blaming. Neither followed the discipline of taking back projections.

We fail on our Soul Path when we are not sufficiently honest. There is a beautiful expression that I associate with my training in Holland with Hans Mensink and Tilke Platteel-Deur, with the Loving Relationship Training given by Sondra Ray and Bob and Mallie Mandel, and with Rebirthing in general. It is *"Going for the highest truth."* Tilke once said, "What I like so much in you, Joy, is that you always go for the highest truth." It was a precious moment and I hope I can always live up to it.

People who walk the Soul Path instinctively search for the highest truth. They cannot be satisfied with anything less. They are profoundly unable and unwilling to make compromises on this subject. Are you like that? Here is an exercise to try:

Going for the Highest Truth

Part 1

- *Ask yourself the following questions and be willing to recognize the thoughts that come up in your mind and the feelings that come up in your body as you do so.*
  —Do I really love my partner as much as I want to think I do?
  —Do I really love my children as much as I want to think I do?
  —Do I really love my parents as much as I want to think I do?

Part 2

- *Make a short list of the qualities or virtues that you value in yourself. Then ask yourself, with regard to each quality:*
  —Am I really as — as I want to think I am?
- *Try this with some of the chapter and section headings in this book.*

Part 3

- *Are there people who have hurt you in some way that you still want to get revenge on? Ask yourself:*
  —Who am I still blaming instead of taking responsibility for what happened to me?
  —How did I let that person hurt me? How can I do it differently now?

Learning

Being honest means having the courage to see when we are "wrong." People who succeed on the Soul Path have the honesty and courage to admit when they are "wrong."

The word "wrong" has frightening connotations. When we are children we are punished for being "wrong." Often we do not understand what was required. Sometimes it is beyond our capacities. We do not feel justly punished, but invalidated in our very being. We are rejected for being "wrong": we want to play with the older children and are not allowed into their group; we want to join a team but are not up to the standard. We lose self-esteem through being "wrong." People are killed for being "wrong": for having the wrong religion or belonging to the wrong tribe, or for committing a crime. How do we as adults find the courage to admit when we are "wrong"?

We are terrifyingly "wrong" so much of the time. We bring up our children as best we can, and yet no parents are completely successful and no children completely satisfied. We are as good to our parents, spouses, and children as we know how to be, and yet some of the time we are careless and hurtful. We do our job as well as we can, and yet sometimes we blunder. We hope always to avoid making mistakes and we make mistakes all the time. We suffer when we make mistakes and we cause suffering when we make mistakes. Being "wrong" is profoundly identified with pain, so we justify and defend ourselves to avoid the pain of admitting it.

If we substitute the concept of *learning* for the concept of "wrongness" we feel safer. Living and learning cannot be separated. Making mistakes is learning how not to do something, which is usually just as valuable as learning how to do it. When we hit a tennis ball badly, we use our knowledge of what went wrong to do it better the next time. When we lose control of our skis, we use our knowledge of what went wrong to improve our technique. Learning is fun. It is opening our horizons, developing our skills and knowledge, confronting challenges, taking risks, *succeeding*. Learning is the question, "What if there is another way?" Learning empowers. We proceed along our Soul Path through learning.

Grace

We do our best. We abide by the rule of not blaming. We take back our projections. We go for the highest truth and are as ethical as we know how to be, and yet there are still things that we fail at, there are still problems we cannot come to the end of, we still have intense suffering for one reason or another. It seems impossible to change what we want to change. It seems impossible to find the way from the darkness to the light. What is not working?

Progress on the Soul Quest is not controllable. We apply ourselves to our particular problem and despite all our efforts we get nowhere with it. No matter what we learn, no matter how many sessions we do or what kind of sessions we do, our problem persists. It is bigger than all of our teachers, therapists, methods, and techniques, and we are helpless before it. Nevertheless we go on working to develop because that is our discipline. Then one day our problem is gone. It has disappeared. No, we did not just receive or give an inspired session. No, we did not just attend an amazing workshop. No, we did not just read the right book. No, someone did not just give us the right advice. Nothing that we can identify changed in our lives. And yet the problem has disappeared. It went so stealthily that it was as if we had never had it at all, and it took us quite a while to realize we were free.

This is our moment of grace; our moment of destiny. It is unexplainable and uncontrollable, transpersonal and transcendent. Even the most gifted therapist could not induce it. For a long while, despite all our efforts, insight was not available and we were unable to progress. Then suddenly, like the sunrise, like the lifting of clouds that reveals the blue sky, like receiving a blessing, we experience our moment of grace and it is given to us to become free.

Walking the Soul Path

Of course we want to succeed at our Soul Quest. Of course we want to live at Soul-level. Of course we want to advance on our Soul Path. We certainly want success in our personal and spiritual development. What does success mean in this context? We imagine that if we learn the rules and play fair we will inevitably win. The Soul Quest is not a game we can win. There is neither competition nor contest on the Soul Path. The question of success is a wrong question.

To look for success on the Soul Quest and calculate what it may be is spiritual materialism, one-upmanship, the Ego-path of comparisons. We have successes, of course, and they are precious and important, otherwise we would not work on our process. We live our lives better; we understand more; we are less confused; we are happier; our relationships are better; our sex life is more fulfilling; we are doing a rewarding job; life makes more sense and contains more joy. Our ability to sense Soul increases. We become clearer about the difference between Ego-level and Soul-level.

But is there an ultimate success?

What could this ultimate success be?

The Soul Quest never comes to an end. Development is never finished and we never are a completed product. We are always traveling along our Soul Path, always on the way. Whatever the route already covered and the work already accomplished, we can always take a further step. Our potential for development is infinite.

What is successful Soul-Questing? Success means working on our Soul Path and applying ourselves to our personal and spiritual development all the time, without ever asking this question.

A Story To End On

A certain swordsman in his declining years said the following:

In one's life, there are levels in the pursuit of study. In the lowest level, a person studies but nothing comes of it, and he feels that both he and others are unskillful. At this point he is worthless. In the middle level he is still useless but is aware of his own insufficiencies and can also see the insufficiencies of others. In a higher level he has pride concerning his own ability, rejoices in praise from others, and laments the lack of ability in his fellows. This man has worth. In the highest level a man has the look of knowing nothing.

These are the levels in general. But there is one transcending level, and this is the most excellent of all. This person is aware of the endlessness of entering deeply into a certain Way and never thinks of himself as having finished. He truly knows his own insufficiencies and never in his whole life thinks that he has succeeded. He has no thoughts of pride but with self-abasement knows the Way to the end. It is said that Master Yagy once remarked, "I do not know the way to defeat others, but the way to defeat myself."

Throughout your life advance daily, becoming more skillful than yesterday, more skillful than today. This is never-ending.

—Yamamoto Tometomo,
The Book of the Samurai Hagakure

Notes

1. Felicitas Goodman, 1990.

2. Quotes from *The Holy Bible* (New International Version, 1973).

3. Stone and Winkelman, 1989.

4. Schapira, 1988.

5. Stanislav and Christina Grof, 1990.

6. Leonard and Laut, *Rebirthing: The Science of Enjoying All of Your Life,* p. 227. See also Sondra Ray, *The Only Diet There Is.*

7. Parts of this chapter have appeared in Manné, 1995.

8. Majjhima-Nikāya III. London: Pali Text Society, 1977, pp. 82f. My translation.

9. Orr & Ray, Leonard & Laut; Albery has a more critical approach.

10. Rebirthers are particularly associated with following the Indian teacher Babaji. See Albery, *How to Feel Reborn,* p. 72 and elsewhere. Many followers of Babaji think that the Rebirthing books do not do justice to their experience of him and are uncomfortable with the way he is presented in them. I am not a follower of Babaji but I do think it is most important to respect the profound experiences that he has been able to evoke in various people. If you are interested in an inspiring book on this subject, I refer you to *Babaji: Shri Haidakhan Wale Baba,* by Gunnel Minett.

11. I am grateful to Bo Wahlstrom for bringing this relationship to my attention.

12. Timmons, 1994.

13. Secretary Gunnel Minett, 6 Middlewatch, Swavesy, GB-Cambridge CH4 5RN.

14. See *Voice Dialogue International*, Vol. 2, #2, pp. 1–2, on the problems that arise when disowned energies are not worked with wisely.

15. Voice Dialogue International, Delos, Inc., 5451 Laurel Canyon Boulevard, #207, Hollywood, California 91607, USA.

RESOURCE GUIDE

International Breathwork Foundation Members

International Breathwork Foundation
Gunnel Minett
International Coordinator, General Secretary
6 Middlewatch
Swavesy
Cambridge CB4 5RN
Great Britain
Tel. +44 1954 230 250
Fax. +44 1954 232 019
E-mail:
100673.655@compuserve.com

Andningspedagogutbildingen
Directors: Lena Kristina Tuulse
and Bo Wahlström
Wäxthuset
Fjäll 6908
760 40 Väddö
Sweden
Tel. +46 175 85 316 17

Association of Irish Rebirthers
Secretary, Catherine Dowling
33 Inchicore Road
Kilmainham
Dublin 8
Ireland

ATMAN
Wilfried Ehrmann
Eichendorfgasse 8/17
1190 Vienna
Austria
Tel. +43 1 369 23 63
Fax. +43 1 369 21 61
E-mail:
106537.3423@compuserve.com

Breathconnection Life Center
Nemi Nath
"Kaivaly Meru"
Lot 1 Kyogle Road
Lilian Rock
NSW 2480
Australia
Tel. +61 66 897 455
Fax. +61 66 897 533
E-mail: breath@om.com.au

The British College of Holistic Breath Therapy
Mary McGlynn
251 Upper Richmond Road
London SW15 6SW
Great Britain
Tel. +44 181 780 0255
Fax. +44 181 785 2398

British Rebirth Society
General Secretary, Berni Riley
22 Rossall Road
Lytham St. Annes
Lancashire FY8 4ES
Great Britain
Tel. +44 1253 739107

C.A.R. Madrid
Armando G. Aguilar
Quemadillo n° 11
28293 Zarzelejo
Madrid
Spain
Tel. +34 1 899 22 83
Fax. +34 1 899 22 83
E-mail: waktion@openbank.es

The Creative Development Foundation
Robin Lawley B.A. Dip.Ed.
Villa Gaia
Parco Delle Rose
Viale S. Ignazio di Loyolo 250E
80131 Napoli
Italy
Tel. +39 81 58781272
Tel./Fax. +39 81 5873894

Foundation Rebirthing—Poland Inspiration Seminars International
Ewa Foley
Kleczewa 47/3
01 – 826 Warszawa
Poland
Tel. +48 22 346 589
Fax. +48 22 341 706

Instituut voor Integratieve Ademtherapie
Hans Mensink and Tilke Platteel-Deur
Chopinstraat 33
6561 EM Groesbeek
Netherlands
Tel. +31 24 39 78 232

Lynne Jenkins, RIHR
Rebirthing Plus Training to IBF Standards
Neuro Linguistic Training, Craniosacral
485 Huron Street, Apt. 403
Toronto, ONT M5R 2R5
Canada
Tel. +1 416 928 2734

Dr. Joy Manné
9 ch. Des. Roches
1009 Pully
Switzerland
Tel. +41 21 729 1636
Fax. +41 21 729 1635
E-mail:JoyManne@swissonline.ch

The Professional Rebirthing School
Diana Roberts
9d Claverton Street
London SW 1V 3AY
Great Britain
Tel./Fax. +44 171 834 6641

Carrie Callahan Stickley
Breathwork, Dreamwork, Voice Dialogue, Ortho-Bionomy
354 Fairmount Road
Fort Lauderdale
Florida, 33326 USA
Tel. +1 954 349 8949

Kylea Taylor
Holotropic Breathwork
P.O. Box 8051
Santa Cruz, CA 95061
USA
Tel. +1 408 429 1732

Transformations Incorporated
Jim Morningstar
4200W Good Hope Road
Milwaukee, WI 53209
USA
Tel. +1 414 351 5770
Fax. +1 414 351 5760
E-mail: Morning7@aol.com

Roger Woolger
see under Past Life Therapy

French Rebirthers Association
President, Carlene Yasak
42, rue des Acacias
75017 Paris
France
Tel. +33 1 47 66 80 74
Fax. +33 1 45 74 84 48

General

Breathwork, Rebirthing
**Instituut voor Integratieve
Ademtherapie**
see above

Buddhist Psychotherapy

AMIDA Trust
David Brazier
53 Grosvenor Place
Newcastle-upon-tyne NE2 2RD
Great Britain
Tel. +44 191 281 5592
E-mail: amida@amida.demon.co.uk

Past Life Therapy
**Instituut voor Integratieve
Ademtherapie**
see above

**Guus Oesterreicher and Alice
Hulscher**
Frans von Mierisstraat 104
1071 SB Amsterdam
Netherlands
Tel. +31 20 676 5013

Woolger Training Seminars
Roger Woolger
Brairwood
Long Wittenham
Oxon, OX14 4QW
Great Britain
Tel. +44 1865 407 996

Primal Work
**The Primal Integration
Programme**
Juliana Brown and Richard
Mowbray
36 Womersley Road
Crouch End
London N8 9AN
Great Britain
Tel./Fax. +44 181 341 7226

Voice Dialogue
**Instituut voor Integratieve
Ademtherapie**
see above

Hal and Sidra Stone
Delos, Inc.
P.O. Box 604
Albion, California 95410
USA
Tel. +1 707 937 4329
Fax. +1 707 937 4119
E-mail: delos@mcn.org
Website: http://delos-inc.com/

BIBLIOGRAPHY

"Knowledge is power." Discernment is not possible without information. This is a selected bibliography of the books that influenced me in my writing of this book. I hope many of them will be interesting to you. The books marked * have been specifically referred to in the text.

Conscious Breathing Techniques, including Rebirthing

* Albery, Nicholas (1985), *How to Feel Reborn: Varieties of Rebirthing Experience—An Exploration of Rebirthing and Associated Primal Therapies, the Benefits and Dangers, the Facts and Fictions.* London: Regeneration Press.

* *Breathe: The International Breathwork Journal,* editor, Robert Moore, 7 Silver Street, Buckfastleigh, Devon TQ 11 0BQ, Great Britain.

Hendricks, Gay (1995), *Conscious Breathing : Breathwork for Health, Stress Release, and Personal Mastery.* New York: Bantam.

Johnson, Don Hanlon, ed. (1995), *Bone, Breath and Gesture: Practices of Embodiment,* Berkeley, California: North Atlantic Books.

* Leonard, Jim, and Phil Laut (1983), *Rebirthing: The Science of Enjoying All of Your Life,* California: Trinity Publications.

Manné, Joy (1994), "Rebirthing, an orphan or a member of the family of psychotherapies?" *Int. J. of Prenatal and Perinatal Psychology and Medicine,* Vol. 6, No.4, pp. 503-517.

(1995) "Rebirthing—Marvelous or Terrible?" *The Therapist: Journal of the European Therapy Studies Institute,* Spring 1995.

(1996) "On teaching physical Immortality." *Breathe: The International Breathwork Journal,* Issue 64.

* Minett, Gunnel (1994), *Breath and Spirit: Rebirthing as a Healing Technique.* London: The Aquarian Press.

*Orr, Leonard, and Sondra Ray (1983), *Rebirthing in the New Age.* Berkeley, California: Celestial Arts. Revised Ed.

*Ray, Sondra (1981), *The Only Diet There Is.* Berkeley, California: Celestial Arts.

Ray, Sondra, and Bob Mandel (1987), *Birth and Relationships: How your Birth Affects your Relationships.* Berkeley, California: Celestial Arts.

*Sky, Michael (1990), *Breathing: Expanding your Power and Energy.* Santa Fe: Bear & Co.

Taylor, Kylea (1994), *The Breathwork Experience: Exploration and Healing in Nonordinary States of Consciousness.* Santa Cruz, California: Hanford Mead.

*Timmons, Beverly H., and Ronald Ley, eds. (1994), *Behavioral and Psychological Approaches to Breathing Disorders.* New York: Plenum.

Energy Medicine

Benor, Daniel J. (1993–) *Healing Research: Holistic Energy Medicine and Spirituality.* Vols. I-IV. München: Helix.

Coghill, Roger (1992), *Electrohealing: Medicine of the Future.* London: Thorsons.

Mason, Keith (1992), *Medicine for the 21st Century: the Key to Healing with Vibrational Medicine.* Shaftesbury, Dorset: Element Books.

Oldfield, Harry, and Roger Coghill (1988), *The Dark Side of the Brain: Major Discoveries in the Use of Kirlian Photography and Electrocrystal Therapy.* Shaftsbury, Dorset: Element Books.

Inner Child

Bradshaw, John (1990), *Home Coming: Reclaiming and Championing your Inner Child,* London: Piatkus.

Hillman, James, and Michael Ventura (1993), *We've Had a Hundred Years of Psychotherapy and the World's Getting Worse.* San Francisco: Harper.

Whitfield, Charles L. (1987), *Healing the Child Within: Discovery and Recovery for Adult Children of Dysfunctional Families.* Deerfield Beach, Florida: Health Communications, Inc. [2nd ed 1989].

Wolinsky, Stephen (1993), *The Dark Side of the Inner Child: The Next Step.* Norfolk, Connecticut: Bramble Books.

Meditation

Dhiravamsa (1975), *The Way of Non-Attachment: The Practice of Insight Meditation.* London: Turnstone Books.

*Trungpa, Chögyam (1973), *Cutting through Spiritual Materialism.* Berkeley, California: Shambhala.

Past Lives

Moody, Raymond A. (1975), *Life after Life: The Investigation of a Phenomenon—Survival of Bodily Death.* New York: Bantam Books.

Netherton, Morris, Ph.D, & Nancy Schiffrin (1978), *Past Lives Therapy.* New York: Ace.

Stevenson, Ian, (1974), *Twenty Cases Suggestive of Reincarnation.* Charlottesville, Va: University Press of Virginia.

*Woolger, Roger (1988), *Other Lives, Other Selves.* New York: Bantam.

Personal and Spiritual Development

Anthony, Dick, Bruce Ecker, and Ken Wilber (1987), *Spiritual Choices: the Problem of Recognizing Authentic Paths to Inner Transformation.* New York: Paragon House Publishers.

*Ferguson, Marilyn (1981), *The Aquarian Conspiracy: Personal and Social Transformation in the 1980s.* Los Angeles: Jeremy P. Tarcher.

Greer, Jane (1992), *Adult Sibling Rivalry: Understanding the Legacy of Childhood.* New York: Fawcett Crest.

Grof, Christina (1993), *A Quest For Wholeness: Attachment, Addiction and the Spiritual Path.* San Francisco: Harper.

Grof, Stanislav (1975), *Realms of the Human Unconscious: Observations from LSD Research.* New York: Viking Press.

(1988), *The Adventure of Self-Discovery: Dimensions of Consciousness and New Perspectives in Psychotherapy and Inner Exploration.* Albany: University of New York Press.

*Grof, Stanislav, and Christina Grof, eds. (1989), *Spiritual Emergency.* Los Angeles: Jeremy P. Tarcher.

*Harner, Michael (1980), *The Way of the Shaman.* New York: Harper and Row.

*Johnson, Robert A. (1989), *HE: Understanding Masculine Psychology.* New York: Harper and Row.

Kramer, Joel, and Diana Alstad (1993), *The Guru Papers: Masks of Authoritarian Power.* Berkeley, California: North Atlantic Books/Frog Ltd.

Kübler-Ross, Elizabeth (1970), *On Death and Dying.* London: Tavistock Publications.

(1979) *Death, the Final Stage of Growth.* Englewood Cliffs, NJ: Prentice-Hall.

Lockhart, Russell A., et al. (1982), *Soul and Money.* Dallas: Spring Publications.

Leboyer, Frédérick (1975), *Birth without Violence.* London: Wildwood House.

Rebirthing—*see appropriate section.*

*Schapira, Laurie Layton (1988), *The Cassandra Complex: Living with Disbelief—a Modern Perspective on Hysteria.* Toronto: InnerCity Books.

Vaughan, Frances (1986), *The Inward Arc: Healing and Wholeness in Psychotherapy and Spirituality.* Boston: Shambhala.

Voice Dialogue—*see appropriate section.*

Wilkinson, Tanya (1996), *Persephone Returns: Victims, Heroes and the Journey from the Underworld.* Berkeley, California: Pagemill Press.

Woolger, Jennifer Barker Woolger, and Roger Woolger (1990), *The Goddess Within.* London: Rider.

Periodicals

ATMAN—*Erste Österreichische Rebirther Zeitung.* Redaktion Wilfried Ehrmann, Clemens Grebner, Eichendorffgasse 8/17, 1190 Vienna, Austria.

Breathe: The International Breathwork Journal, editor, Robert Moore, 7 Silver Street, Buckfastleigh, Devon TQ 11 0BQ, Great Britain.

The Inner Door, Quarterly Newsletter of the Association for Holotropic Breathwork International, P.O. Box 7167, Santa Cruz, CA 95061-7169, USA.

Journal of Transpersonal Psychology, P.O. Box 4437, Stanford, California 94305, USA.

Journal of Humanistic Psychology, 325 Ninth Street, San Francisco, California 94103, USA.

Pre and Peri-Natal Psychology Association, 1600 Prince Street, #509, Alexandria, VA 22314, USA.

The Therapist, Journal of the European Therapy Studies Institute, ETSI, The Office, 7 Chapel Road, Worthing, West Sussex BN11 1EG, Great Britain.

What Doctors Don't Tell You, 4 Wallace Road, London N1 2PG, Great Britain.

Primal Health Research, Primal Health Research Center, 59 Roderick Road, London NW3 2NP, Great Britain. Fax. +44 (0)171 2675123.

Somatics, 1516 Grant Avenue, Suite 212, Novato, California 94945, USA.

Sexual Abuse

Accuracy about Abuse. P.O. Box 3125, London NW3 5QB, Great Britain. Contact Marjorie Orr, Tel. +44 171 431 5339, Fax. +44 171 433 3101, e-mail: morr@aaastar.demon.co.uk.

*Bass, Ellen, and Laura Davis (1992), *The Courage to Heal: A Guide for Women Survivors of Child Sexual Abuse.* New York: Harper Perennial.

The False Memory Syndrome Foundation, 3401 Market Street, Suite 130, Philadelphia, PA 19204, USA. Tel. (215) 387-1865.

*Goldstein, Eleanor, and Kevin Farmer (1993), *True Stories of False Memories.* Florida: SIRS Books.

Rutter, Peter, M.D. (1991), *Sex in the Forbidden Zone.* New York: Fawcett Crest.

Yapko, Michael D., Ph.D. (1994), *Suggestions of Abuse: True and False Memories of Childhood Sexual Trauma.* New York: Simon & Schuster.

The Shadow

Bly, Robert (1988), *A Little Book on the Human Shadow,* Shaftesbury, Dorset: Element Books.

Johnson, Robert A. (1991), *Owning Your Own Shadow: Understanding the Dark Side of the Psyche.* San Francisco: Harper.

Zweig, Connie and Jeremiah Abrams, eds. (1991), *Meeting the Shadow: the Hidden Power of the Dark Side of Human Nature.* Los Angeles: Jeremy P. Tarcher.

Soul Path

Bolen, Jean Shinoda (1994), *Crossing to Avalon: a Woman's Midlife Pilgrimage.* San Francisco: Harper.

Boltwood, Geoff (1994), The Messenger: Journey of a Spiritual Teacher. London: Piatkus.

Conscious Breathing/Rebirthing—*see appropriate section.*

Grossinger, Richard (1995), *Planet Medicine, Volume I, Origins; Volume II, Modalities.* Berkeley, California: North Atlantic Books.

(1996) *New Moon.* Berkeley, California: North Atlantic Books.

* *The Holy Bible* (New International Version, 1973). London: Hodder and Stoughton.

Ital, Gerda (1987), *The Master, the Monks and I.* Northamptonshire, England: Crucible.

(1990), *On the Way to Satori: A Woman's Experience of Enlightenment.* Dorset: Element Books.

* Minett, Gunnel (1986), *Babaji: Shri Haidakhan Wale Baba.* Stockholm, Sweden: Samba Sada Shiva Dham Ashram.

Sardello, Robert (1992), *Facing the World with Soul: The Reimagination of Modern Life.* Hudson: Lindisfarne Press. [Harper Perennial edition, 1994]

Stone, Hal (1985), *Embracing Heaven and Earth: A Personal Odyssey.* Marina del Rey, CA: DeVorss and Company.

Tweedie, Irene (1978), *The Chasm of Fire: A Woman's Experience of Liberation through the Teaching of a Sufi Master.* Dorset: Element Books.

Voice Dialogue—*see appropriate section.*

* Yamamoto Tometomo (1979), *The Book of the Samurai Hagakure.* Translated by William Scott Wilson. New York and Tokyo: Kodansha.

Subtle Energy

Brennan, Barbara Ann (1988), *Hands of Light: A Guide to Healing through the Human Energy-Field.* New York: Bantam Books.

(1993), *Light Emerging: The Journey of Personal Healing.* New York: Bantam.

Joy, W. Brugh, M.D. (1979), *Joy's Way: A Map for the Transformational Journey.* Los Angeles: Jeremy P. Tarcher.

Keen, Linda (1989), *Epanouissement psychique*. Paris: Guy Trédaniel Editeur.

Klimo, Jon (1988), *Channeling: Investigations on Receiving Information from Paranormal Sources*. Berkeley: North Atlantic Books, 1997.

Krieger, Dolores (1986), *The Therapeutic Touch: How to Use Your Hands to Help or to Heal*. New York: Prentice Hall Press.

Therapy

* Brazier, David (1995), *Zen Therapy*. London: Constable.

* Breggin, Peter (1992), *Toxic Psychiatry*. London: Fontana.

Conscious Breathing Techniques—*see appropriate section.*

Epstein, Mark (1995), *Thoughts without a Thinker: Psychotherapy from the Buddhist Perspective*. New York: Basic Books.

Gendlin, E. T. (1981), *Focussing*. New York: Bantam Books.

Greene, Liz (1985), *The Astrology of Fate*. London: Mandala.

* Hobson, Robert F. (1985), *Forms of Feeling: The Heart of Psychotherapy*. London: Tavistock.

Jung, Carl Gustav (1963), *Memories, Dreams, Reflections*. London: Fontana, 1989.

Maslow, Abraham H. (1968), *Towards a Psychology of Being*. New York: D. Van Nostrand Company. [2nd ed.]

(1971), *The Further Reaches of Human Nature*. New York: Viking Press.

Miller, Alice (1981), *The Drama of the Gifted Child: Facing Childhood Injuries*. New York: Basic Books.

(1987), *For Your Own Good: The Roots of Violence in Child-Rearing*. London: Virago.

(1984), *Thou Shalt Not Be Aware: Society's Betrayal of the Child*. London: Pluto Press.

(1990), *The Untouched Key: Tracing Childhood Trauma in Creativity and Destructiveness*. London: Virago.

(1991), *Banished Knowledge: Facing Childhood Injuries*. London: Virago.

(1991), *Breaking down the Wall of Silence: To Join the Waiting Child*. London: Virago.

* Mowbray, Richard (1995), *The Case against Psychotherapy Registration: A Conservation Issue for the Human Potential Movement.* London: Trans Marginal Press.

Nouwen, Henri J.M. (1979), *The Wounded Healer.* New York: Doubleday.

Odent, Michel (1984), *Birth Reborn.* New York: Pantheon.

Rebirthing—*see Conscious Breathing Techniques.*

Reinhart, Melanie (1989), *Chiron and the Healing Journey: An Astrological and Psychological Perspective.* London: Arkana,

Rowan, John (1988), *Ordinary Ecstasy: Humanistic Psychology in Action.* London: Routledge.

(1990), *Subpersonalities: The People Inside Us.* London: Routledge.

(1993), *Discover your Subpersonalities: Our Inner World and the People in It.* London: Routledge.

(1993a), *The Transpersonal: Psychotherapy and Counselling.* London: Routledge.

Sheehy, Gail (1976), *Passages: Predictable Crises of Adult Life.* New York: Bantam.

(1995) *New Passages: Mapping Your Life Across Time.* New York: Ballantine Books.

* Siegel, Bernie (1986) *Love, Medicine and Miracles: Lessons Learned about Self-Healing From a Surgeon's Experience with Exceptional Patients.* New York: Harper and Row.

* Simonton, O. Carl, Stephanie Matthews-Simonton, and James Creighton (1978), *Getting Well Again: A Step-By-Step, Self-Help Guide to Overcoming Cancer for Patients and Their Families.* Los Angeles: Jeremy P. Tarcher.

Verny, Thomas, ed. (1987), *Pre- and Perinatal Psychology: An Introduction.* New York: Human Sciences Press.

Voice Dialogue—*see appropriate section.*

Voice Dialogue

Stone, Hal, and Sidra Winkelman (1985), *Embracing Our Selves: Voice Dialogue Manual.* Marina del Rey, California: Devorss & Company.

(1989), *Embracing Each Other: Relationship as Teacher, Healer and Guide.* San Rafael, California: New World Library.

Stone, Hal, and Sidra Stone (1993), *Embracing your Inner Critic: Turning Self-Criticism into a Creative Asset.* San Francisco: Harper.

Stone, Sidra, (1997), *The Shadow King: The Invisible Force That Holds Women Back*. Mill Valley, California: Nataraj Publishing.

Voice Dialogue International, Newsletter of the World Voice Dialogue Community. Delos, Inc., 5451 Laurel Canyon Boulevard, #207, N. Hollywood, California 91607, USA.

Miscellaneous

* Goodman, Felicitas (1990), *Where the Spirits Ride the Wind: Trance Journeys and Other Ecstatic Experiences*. Bloomington: Indiana University Press.

Majjhima-Nikāya III, translated by I. B. Horner as *The Middle Length Sayings,* Vol. III. London: Pali Text Society, 1977.

Manné, Joy (1990), "Categories of Sutta in the Pāli Nikāyas and their implications for our appreciation of the Buddhist Teachings and Literature." *Journal of the Pali Text Society,* XV (1990), pp. 29-87.

INDEX